Legacy

THE KREIELSHEIMER FOUNDATION

Legacy

THE KREIELSHEIMER FOUNDATION

Edited by Paul Dorpat
Preface by Donald L. Johnson

ESSAYS BY

Paul Dorpat

Shelia Farr

Michael James

Genevieve McCoy

Jean Sherrard

THE KREIELSHEIMER REMAINDER FOUNDATION

in association with

UNIVERSITY OF WASHINGTON PRESS
SEATTLE & LONDON

University of Washington Press

P.O. Box 50096, Seattle, WA 98145

www.washington.edu/uwpress

Library of Congress Cataloging-in-Publication Data
Legacy : the Kreielsheimer Foundation : edited by Paul Dorpat ; preface by Donald L. Johnson ; essays by Paul Dorpat [et. al.].—1st ed.
      p. cm.
Includes bibliographical references and index.
ISBN 0-295-98603-4 (pbk. : alk. paper)
1. Kreielsheimer Foundation—Art patronage. 2. Art patronage—Washington (State)—Seattle—History—20th century. 3. Arts, American—Washington (State)—Seattle—20th century.
I. Dorpat, Paul.
NX712.K74L44 2006
700.79'797772—dc22   2005031049

The paper used in this publication is acid-free and meets the minimum requirements of American National Standard for Information Sciences—Permanence of Paper for Printed Library Materials, ANSI Z39.48-1984.

Contents

"To give away money is an easy matter and in any man's power. But to decide to whom to give it, and how large and when, and for what purpose and how, is neither in every man's power, nor an easy matter. Hence it is that such excellence is rare, praiseworthy, and noble."
—ARISTOTLE

Leo Kreielsheimer, ca. 1960

Preface

On July 25, 1975, Leo T. Kreielsheimer placed his signature on his Last Will and Testament. Two months later on September 20, 1975, he passed away. These events created the Kreielsheimer Foundation. After providing for his family, Leo Kreielsheimer left the bulk of his fortune to the Foundation. In 1980, his wife, Greye McCormick Kreielsheimer, died, and she likewise left the bulk of her estate to the Foundation. When distributions from Leo and Greye's estates were completed, the Foundation received between $22 million and $23 million.

Leo Kreielsheimer's will provided that the Foundation must conclude its active philanthropic grants twenty-five years after his death. Consequently, the last grants were made on September 20, 2000, although distributions continue from perpetual endowment grants and funds held in trust awaiting the occurrence of preconditions to the distribution of those grants.

In addition to the twenty-five-year term limitation, Leo Kreielsheimer's will contained three other notable provisions: (1) Grants were to be rather narrowly focused—in essence, they were limited to the arts and education fields. (2) The administration of the Foundation was to be quite simple. There were to be only two trustees: Seafirst Bank, later to become Bank of America (the "Bank Trustee"), and Charles F. Osborn (the "Individual Trustee"), who was Leo Kreielsheimer's personal attorney. (3) If the Bank Trustee and the Individual Trustee disagreed over whether a grant should be made or not, the Individual Trustee's decision was to be controlling. The practical effect of this last provision was to place primary responsibility for trust asset investment and management in Seafirst Bank and primary responsibility for grant making in Charles Osborn.

Charles Osborn was a partner in the prominent Seattle law firm of Bogle & Gates. He was a brilliant man, specializing in the tax and estate planning fields. As Leo Kreielsheimer's personal attorney and confidant, Osborn clearly played a key role in assisting Leo Kreielsheimer in the creation and structure of the Kreielsheimer Foundation.

Following the settlement of Leo and Greye's estates, the Foundation was able to make its first charitable distribution in 1981. Charles Osborn was a fiscal conservative. Consequently, during much of the 1980s, except for a few large gifts, he limited distributions to the minimum required by the tax laws and regulations applicable to charitable trusts. This policy of limited distributions, coupled with wise and fortuitous investment decisions, enabled the trustees to build the Foundation's assets so significantly that in excess of $100 million was given or committed to the community by September 2000.

Sadly, Charles Osborn succumbed to a six-year battle with cancer on August 31, 1992. Leo Kreielsheimer's will provided that if Osborn could not serve as co-trustee "he shall be succeeded by Donald L. Johnson." And so on September 1, 1992, I became the Individual Trustee and served in that role for the ensuing eight years.

On September 1,1957, fresh out of law school, I had joined Bogle & Gates, then the largest law firm in Seattle. Eerily, to me at least, thirty-five years later virtually to the day, my career, as a practical matter, changed from that of a lawyer specializing in business law to a Kreielsheimer trustee. During those years, one of my first mentors was Charles Osborn. Along with my partner and dear friend, Max Kaminoff, they were instrumental in influencing my career as a lawyer, and eventually as a Kreielsheimer trustee. I worked closely with Leo Kreielsheimer from the late 1960s until his death, and developed a great affection for his kindly and delightful personality.

The story or, rather, some of the many stories of the Kreielsheimer philanthropy are told in *Legacy*.

The $22–$23 million originally placed in the trust seems, by today's standards of the mega-rich, rather modest, but as you will learn in the pages ahead the funds received from the Kreielsheimer estate through fortuitous investments grew to in excess of $100 million. I am told that much good was accomplished for the Washington and Alaska communities by Leo and Greye Kreielsheimer's generosity. It is my hope that this book will help motivate younger members of our community with the means to do so, to emulate the Kreielsheimers.

The Foundation's focus on the arts and arts education provided, and continues to provide through endowment and lasting capital grants, support to the cultural component that is essential to a meaningful and full life. Too often the arts are relegated to a secondary position by the public and private sectors of the community when economic resources are allocated.

I want to express my gratitude to the many individuals and institutions in the Washington and Alaska communities whose generous help (ranging from a simple bit of sage advice to the work of philanthropic comrades who on more than one occasion said, in effect, "Don, if you'll make this grant, I'll match it") has been invaluable. I particularly want to thank my co-trustee, the Bank of America, and its predecessor, SeaFirst Bank, especially Bruce H. "Gus" Cleveland for his steadfast and always reliable help. Kudos also to the Seattle investment firm of Badgley, Phelps & Bell, especially Warren Bell and Steve Phelps, for their astute investment advice.

My deep appreciation also goes to:

In the public sector: former Governor and Senator Dan Evans; former Governor Gary Locke; former Seattle Mayor Paul Schell; King County Council Members Louise Miller and Larry Phillips; Seattle City Council Members Sue Donaldson and Jan Drago; and one of the most dedicated public servants I have encountered, Seattle Center Director Virginia Anderson.

In the public education sector: former University of Washington Presidents Bill Gerberding and Richard McCormick, and to Western Washington University President Karen Morse.

Community philanthropists: especially the Alvord family (Buster, Nancy, Chap, and Eve, and Katharyn Alvord Gerlich); Sally Behnke and her family; Jack and Becky Benaroya; Jeff and Susan Brotman; the late Priscilla (Patsy) Collins; David and Jane Lang Davis; Kemper Freeman, Jr., and his family; Marian McCaw Garrison and her sons; Bill Gates (father and son); Marshall Hatch; Anne Gould Hauberg; Bill Jenkins and Ann Ramsay-Jenkins; John and Laurel Nesholm; James and Sherri Raisbeck; the late Elmer and Mary Louise Rasmuson (Alaska); Sam and Gladys Rubinstein; Jon and Mary Shirley; the late Kayla Skinner; Arlene Wright; Bagley and Virginia Wright; and many others.

In the corporate community: Boeing (especially Phil Condit, Frank Shrontz, and Ron Woodard), Safeco (especially Julie Anderson), and Washington Mutual (especially Deanna Oppenheimer).

All of our generally underpaid and dedicated arts administrators and artistic directors, especially Speight Jenkins and the late Kathy Magiera of Seattle Opera, Gerard Schwarz and Deborah Card of the Seattle Symphony, Mimi Gates of the Seattle Art Museum, Richard Andrews of the Henry Art Gallery, Sharon Ott and Ben Moore of the Seattle Repertory Theatre, Susan Baird Trapnell of ACT, Laura Penn of Intiman Theatre, Melissa Hines of the Empty Space Theatre, and Linda Hartzell of Seattle Children's Theatre.

Peter Donnelly, producing director of the Seattle Repertory Theatre for eighteen years and, until his retirement on December 31, 2005, president of the ArtsFund, formerly Corporate Council for the Arts; another book could be written about Peter's tireless efforts to aid the arts and those who work to uplift the arts.

My partners, associates, and friends at the late, great Bogle & Gates (which dissolved in 1999 after 108 years of service as a preeminent law firm in the community); especially James F. Tune, Irwin L. Treiger, Mark Paben, Kimberly Osenbaugh, Elaine Spencer, and, of course, the late Charles F. Osborn.

Harriet Osborn, widow of Charles F. Osborn, and the late Olivia Kreielsheimer.

My office assistants, especially Jo Van Krevelen and Sandy Fry.

And finally, thanks to my understanding and tolerant family — my dear wife, Dorothy (Dottie to her many friends), and our daughters, Kimberly, Kristin, and Karin.

It would take more than the space allotted here to name everyone whose help I have sought over the years. For such omissions I apologize, but please know of my deep appreciation. Without all of you it would clearly not have been possible to implement the many opportunities afforded by the Kreielsheimers' generosity. Many of you appear in the pages of this book.

DONALD L. JOHNSON
SEATTLE, JANUARY 2006

Introduction

The publishing of *Legacy* comes more than five years after the Kreielsheimer Foundation came to the end scheduled for it by founders Leo and Greye Kreielsheimer a quarter century earlier in 1975. The interval has allowed the authors time to review the contributions of the Foundation and to now share a few of its many stories, while reflecting on the Kreielsheimer legacy. The five writers involved have all been active in the arts as artists and/or as reporters and critics.

In chapter 1, Mike James describes the considerable benefits that the Foundation distributed to performing groups in the musical arts. Through his distinguished career as a television reporter, anchor, and producer, James has extended the regional coverage of the arts—especially during his many years with KING broadcasting.

The Foundation's contributions to the visual arts are Sheila Farr's focus in chapter 2. Art critic for the *Seattle Times*, Farr is author of several books on Northwest artists, including *Fay Jones* (2000), *Leo Kenney: A Retrospective* (2000), and *James Martin: Art Rustler at the Rivoli* (2001), all published by the University of Washington Press. She is also a poet, whose work has appeared nationally in a number of journals as well as a book, *The Snake Song* (Signpost Press, 1994).

In chapter 3, Jean Sherrard details the considerable role the Foundation had in supporting local theater. Sherrard's knack for the subject springs from a life of acting, directing, and producing radio theater (Globe Radio Repertory). The Poetry Society of America first recognized his signal pith and vinegar when they awarded him Best in Show at the tender age of sixteen.

Dance is the subject of chapter 4. Author Genevieve McCoy has a lifelong interest in dance both as a patron and in practice. She also gives the book some academic alloy—she teaches history at the University of Washington. With Paul Dorpat, McCoy is coauthor of *Building Washington: A History of Washington State Public Works* (Tartu Publications, 1998).

Paul Dorpat completes *Legacy* with a variety of thematic chapters. Inevitably, Dorpat's contributions will advert to some of the same subjects treated by the other contributors. Dorpat has authored several books on regional history and since 1981 has written a weekly column for the *Seattle Times*. He is also responsible for organizing both the writing of the book and its sections.

Legacy: The Kreielsheimer Foundation concludes with an appendix that lists the Foundation's many grantees.

Approached dramatically, the book is a charmed comedy about the exhilarating good fortune of a foundation dedicated to funding arts and education through years made bountiful by a soaring storybook economic scene. The investment side was an exceedingly bullish ride, and, since the entire gallop of growing and giving for Leo T. and Greye M. Kreielsheimer was done posthumously, it was their hand-picked trustees, Charles F. Osborn and Donald L. Johnson, who held on during the great roundup of wealth and its distribution.

Two lessons learned from the Foundation should be noted in this introduction. The Kreielsheimer philanthropy is not finished. Having concentrated more than $100 million in the support of regional art and education (mostly art education), the work of the Kreielsheimer Foundation will continue to resonate for years to come. That Leo Kreielsheimer, a witty but modest cannery owner, was chosen in 2001 as one of the 150 most influential persons in the history of the city by Seattle's Sesquicentennial Committee is a testimony to the great work of his and his wife's namesake foundation and only indirectly to their knack for catching salmon. Leo and Greye might have continued to multiply their wealth in real estate and other securities. Instead they chose to bequeath most of their fortune to the delights of the arts. So the second lesson is in their example. It is the candid hope of those creating this chronicle—and really part of its intended purpose—to encourage others to do the same. Don Johnson explains, "I hope the Kreielsheimer Foundation story will motivate others to get involved in supporting the arts. Everyone looks at the great work of the Gateses and the Allens, but it is not just the mega-rich who can help. There are many others with deep pockets. They can make a tremendous difference."

Although, as mandated by the Kreielsheimer will, the last trustee closed the doors of the Foundation on September 20, 2000, twenty-five years after the death of Leo Kreielsheimer, to the contributors to this book those doors were always open. As one, we wish to thank Don Johnson and Jo Van Krevelen, the last of Johnson's assistants, for their hospitality and good-humored help. Fortunately both trustees—with the considerable help of their assistants like Sandy Fry and Van Krevelen—were conscientious recordkeepers. At closing time every permutation of the Foundation's philanthropy was figured and refigured in helpful lists, including the most obvious: the alphabetical listing of grantees that is the final offering of this book, following the text (see Appendix).

As the book's five contributors soon learned, the well-ordered files of the Foundation are sources of many delightful memories for the last trustee. Don Johnson is the obvious link to the whole history of the Foundation, having worked closely with both Leo Kreielsheimer and Charles Osborn long before the Foundation was created and perhaps even imagined. All of us conversed with Don on the details of our subjects. We repeatedly met individually with him in the Kreielsheimer office on the third floor of the Century Building, one block west of the Seattle Center campus. The writers spent so much time listening to Don—and often, thankfully, recording him—that we may be considered as five Boswells to this Johnson.

In the Kreielsheimer office overlooking Don Johnson's desk is a cherished photograph of opera diva Beverly Sills. It was taken during her 1994 visit

Left to right: Don Johnson, Dorothy Johnson, Peter Donnelly, and Beverly Sills at the 1994 ArtsFund reception

to Seattle to address the annual luncheon of the ArtsFund, then called
the Corporate Council for the Arts. Something the director of Lincoln
Center said during her keynote remarks expressed for the trustee what the
Kreielsheimer Foundation was all about. Don Johnson recalls she said,
in effect, "Life is shades of gray until the arts are infused—then it
becomes color!"

The name "Kreielsheimer" divides opinion. Is it more difficult to
spell or pronounce? Olivia Kreielsheimer gently reminded Don Johnson
that it is correctly pronounced "Kryls-hymer." But, once learned, the meter
of the name can be a delight to recite, especially so for the many who have
been benefited by its presence. And unless you are a visitor from afar, the
charmed circle of the Kreielsheimer largess almost certainly includes you—
the reader—whether you are an artist, arts administrator, or one who
admires the work of both.

PAUL DORPAT
SEATTLE, 2006

Part I

The Major Arts

1 Music

Michael James

Seattle Symphony

"It was a joke to talk about building a concert hall." That's how Deborah Card, executive director of the Seattle Symphony Orchestra, remembers the harsh financial reality that engulfed her when she took over the job in November 1992. No wonder. The Symphony had, in her words, "hideous cash flow problems": an accumulated deficit of $2.2 million, a planned season deficit of more than $900,000, and outstanding bank loans totaling $1.4 million. Card checked the cash flows each day to see which vendors could be paid, and how much. The orchestra owed virtually every printer in town, so none of them would print season renewal brochures. Ron Woodard, a Boeing executive who chaired the Board of Trustees in the 1990s, says the Symphony was "essentially bankrupt."

In December 1992, Mary Ann Champion, president of the Symphony Board and interim executive director for most of that year, carried that gloomy message with her into the Two Union Square office of Bogle & Gates, where she had an appointment with the Kreielsheimer Foundation's new trustee, Don Johnson. Champion wanted Foundation money to help the orchestra cut that huge deficit, to match a significant debt reduction contribution from PONCHO (Patrons of Northwest Civic, Cultural, and Charitable Organizations), and to qualify for a million-dollar National Arts Stabilization Grant that could save the Seattle Symphony. She says now she would have done almost anything to get help. Champion arrived to see Johnson an hour before the annual Christmas party at Johnson's law firm. Inside his office, away from the celebrations, she burst into tears. "I had to plead and beg," she remembers. "I was so upset and worried that we were going to crumble that I pulled out all the stops. Desperate people do desperate things, and I had to get out of that hole or we were going to crumble." Champion could hardly know that day, that within six months the orchestra's shaky finances would begin to stabilize, and the idea of a concert hall would no longer be a joke.

The Kreielsheimer Foundation's connection with the Seattle Symphony, and with the dream of a concert hall, had begun years before, when Johnson's predecessor as co-trustee, Charles Osborn, purchased a block of land near the Seattle Center, just across the street from the Opera House. Osborn had detested the idea of a downtown art museum (a "blighted, high-risk" location, he argued), and offered the Mercer Street block to the board of the Seattle Art Museum as an incentive to abandon their plans for downtown. When the museum's trustees rejected the Foundation offer, Osborn turned his focus to the Seattle Symphony, and the need for a dedicated concert hall.

There wasn't much argument about the need; the Ballet, Opera, and Symphony were practically falling over each other inside the multipurpose Seattle Center Opera House, perfectly described by the *New York Times* as "a drably functional theater left over from the 1962 World's Fair." One study called the stage entrance "a great revolving door." The frantic schedule (the Opera House was booked almost every day of the year) forced the orchestra players to rehearse in a crowded side room, away from the main stage. "That was a huge deal for me," says Music Director Gerard Schwarz, wincing as he remembers the sound of that room. "That was so horrible on everybody's hearing. It was a terrible place for us to work." The need for change was confirmed in a 1987 feasibility study funded by the Kreielsheimer Foundation. In its final report, the Collins Group found the Opera House "overbooked," a place where "artistic growth is stifled." Collins recommended development of the Kreielsheimer property as a concert hall with the Symphony as its major tenant.

In a letter dated April 14, 1986, the Foundation deeded the Mercer Street block to the city for "cultural purposes," with the stipulation that work had to begin within four years. This was typical Osborn; when he acted, he wanted action in return. Setting a deadline, he thought, would give the Symphony, and the community, an incentive to get something done. The Orchestra, though, while it might dream of a concert hall, of escaping the artistic traffic jam at the Opera House, couldn't imagine how to make it happen. The Symphony had virtually no endowment, which made each year a never-ending struggle just to survive financially. During his study of concert hall feasibility, Richard Collins had warned against any *public* talk about a concert hall, noting that it would be "a serious public relations gaffe," given the Symphony's weak financial condition. Osborn, while willing to finance concert hall studies, was adamant "that the Foundation would not contribute anything for the payment of the debt of the Symphony, which is the result of poor management over a period of years." What he *was* willing to finance, however, and his personal zeal in doing so, built the foundation for the Seattle Symphony's remarkable renaissance in the 1990s.

Osborn, through the Foundation, paid for the feasibility study, which confirmed the Kreielsheimer site as well-suited for a concert hall. He paid for early architectural studies by LMN Architects (then known as Loschky Marquardt & Nesholm) that developed the essential concert hall design later adapted to the Benaroya Hall site downtown. He took Schwarz's advice and brought in acoustician Dr. Cyril Harris to develop the acoustic shape of a new concert hall. Osborn also formed a Citizens Advisory Committee, including several symphony musicians, to work with the architects and paid for travel all over the country so the group could study other concert halls. Most of all, with letters, phone calls, and personal meetings, he kept constant pressure on the Symphony leadership and the city to *act*.

In one characteristic example, a May 1988 letter to Symphony Executive Director Ed Birdwell, Osborn complains about the lukewarm attitude of Symphony board leaders Richard Cooley and Sam Stroum, grumbles that they wouldn't display a model of the proposed concert hall at the board's annual dinner, and writes that "it is futile for the Kreielsheimer Foundation to push the project further without strong support from the leaders of the Symphony." Later, in a 1990 letter demanding commitments from the city, he warns that an extension of the looming deadline is "unlikely." Osborn quarreled with almost everyone in pursuing the concert hall idea, but no one doubts that his persistence made a crucial difference.

Oboist John DeJarnatt, one of the Symphony musicians who went on those trips to other concert halls, says Osborn kept the concert hall idea afloat at a point when no one else was talking about it, a time "when nobody was thinking beyond the paycheck next week." Birdwell would say, years later, "Charlie, virtually alone, kept the flame alive in the darkest days." In 1988, shortly after LMN Architects presented their Kreielsheimer-

THE SCORE

VOTE YES FOR SEATTLE CENTER ON MAY 28

King County and Seattle voters will have the chance to vote for the redevelopment of Seattle Center including a new concert hall for the Seattle Symphony.

AN EIGHTY YEAR OLD DREAM

The idea of a new concert hall has been a dream of the Seattle Symphony and the region for over eighty years. Now that dream is close to becoming reality.

BUILDING A CONCERT HALL

Managing Director Ed Birdwell discusses the process of building a new concert hall for the community.

SEATTLE SYMPHONY

LMN architects' 1989 rendering of the proposed new concert hall on Mercer Street

funded design concept for the concert hall.* Melinda Bargreen, the influential music critic at the *Seattle Times*, wrote Osborn a personal note to congratulate him "on being the one person in Seattle with the vision to get this fine project started." Conductor Schwarz, who lived through all the financial crises—salary freezes, cancelled programs, shortened seasons—that made the concert hall seem like a wistful and distant dream, says that Osborn and the Kreielsheimer Foundation saved the concert hall vision. "Without them," he says, "it would have died many, many times."

Timing, that mysterious convergence of opportunity and feasibility and desire, is often crucial in great civic projects. Schwarz says the great gift of Osborn and the Foundation was *time*. Osborn's doggedness on the concert hall "gave us time to sell the idea. If you say to someone, we need a new concert hall in this town, that's not something that happens overnight. The community has to buy it, the mayor has to buy it, the governor has to buy it, the philanthropic community has to buy it. By Charlie getting us started with it, we had time for it to sink in." Mark Reddington, the principal architect on the project, both the early design and at Benaroya, agrees. "The process through which that project developed, with Kreielsheimer commissioned studies, allowed us to develop a symphonic hall in a way

* The rendering was presented in a brochure with a brilliant binding that became known as "The Red Book."

that probably could never have happened otherwise. Charlie understood that. The Foundation gave us the time. We had the time to dream."

But the realization of the dream would not come in Charlie Osborn's lifetime. He fought with the Symphony leadership over the need to act, accused them of dragging their feet, of indifference to opportunity, but they had the reality of a continuing budget crisis and could not, credibly, lead a concert hall campaign. He reacted angrily when a new Concert Hall Task Force, convened by Mayor Charles Royer in 1989, explored conversion of the Paramount Theater into a symphony concert hall (an infuriated Osborn vowed "not to give a penny" to such a project). The Task Force eventually recommended the Kreielsheimer site, and the Foundation promptly extended the deadline for concert hall action. But when a concert hall levy failed in May of 1991 (city voters approved, but county voters rejected the plan), the Osborn dream seemed at an end. Even now, Gerard Schwarz remembers one of his last conversations with Ed Birdwell, just before the levy vote. He recalls saying, "Ed, let's hope we win, but if we lose, what do we do?" Ed said, "Jerry, just pray we win."

But the levy went down. Spending on that campaign had pushed the Symphony another $750 thousand in debt. Birdwell eventually resigned as executive director. The Orchestra cut sixteen concerts, reduced staff, froze musician wages, and even gave up coffee in the office. The endowment campaign, which would have been part of a concert hall capital campaign, appeared dead. The concert hall vision had become, as philanthropist Sam Stroum would say to Schwarz on the telephone, "a pipe dream." Still, Osborn would not concede. He peppered Symphony and civic leaders, even as his own health failed, with letters insisting that someone come forward. He demanded leadership, and threatened to take the Kreielsheimer property back. In a letter just two months after the concert hall vote, Osborn was blunt as ever: "The time has come to decide whether this project is to proceed or to be put on hold indefinitely."

Osborn did agree, after a personal request from Mayor Norm Rice, to extend the deadline for concert hall action another year. He warned, though, that the extension would be the last, "unless there is strong evidence that the concerned parties are working together and are close to a final plan of action." The decision on that next extension, though, would fall to Don Johnson. Charles Osborn died of cancer in August 1992.

Johnson, Osborn's successor as co-trustee of the Kreielsheimer Foundation, knew he couldn't give up the concert hall dream; too much hope and time and money had been spent. Too much of Charlie was there. In December 1992, Johnson extended the action deadline on the concert hall block for one more year, on condition the Symphony show progress in fund-raising, and that the city make progress toward public funding of a concert hall. He wasn't sure, though, how to react to Mary Ann Champion's emotional plea for help in his office that day. Osborn had set a fundamental rule for the Foundation — no grants for operating expenses, no cash to cover deficits — and Johnson (who would make important exceptions later on) intended to honor Charlie's precedent. What he did, though, in a creative stroke that set the tone for Johnson's Kreielsheimer leadership, put the Symphony on the road back.

Johnson gave the orchestra, not cash but a challenge — an endowment grant of $1 million that the Symphony had to match dollar for dollar. Johnson's twist on the payout was what made all the difference. Under the Foundation proposal, the orchestra could use the first $200,000 raised for the grant to reduce the deficit, to help the Symphony qualify for that National Arts Stabilization Fund money. Most important, for Symphony Executive Director Deborah Card, it sent a signal to the philanthropic community in Seattle. "I think this community didn't trust the Symphony to really mean what it was saying — we're in trouble, we need help, please come to our rescue — and this gift indicated that we had a real plan for a solution." Card admits that she would have preferred outright cash, instead of Johnson's carrot-and-stick approach, but the Kreielsheimer plan worked. It gave legitimacy to the Symphony's deficit reduction plan, it brought in new money, it made a recently adopted strategic plan credible, and it forced a new budget and fund-raising discipline on the orchestra. Mary Ann Champion, who sent Johnson a personal note, saying she was "thrilled" at his response, believes the Kreielsheimer gift, while small in actual dollars, set in motion a chain of events that catapulted the Symphony into a new concert hall and a new era. "If the Kreielsheimer Foundation had not given me that money on that given day of desperation, and we then didn't get the Arts Stabilization Fund money and we weren't able to balance the budget and we weren't able to reduce our loan at the bank and we weren't able to announce to the community that we had a deficit reduction campaign going, I am convinced that the top wouldn't have kept spinning, and we wouldn't have become stable, and therefore Jack Benaroya would never have made his gift."

Benaroya's astonishing 1993 gift of $15.8 million, at that point the largest private charitable gift in state history, took the concert hall, at a stroke, from Sam Stroum's "pipe dream" to plausible reality. Schwarz says now, "That told me it was going to happen. Absolutely. What we needed was that gift. Without that first major gift, it would never happen." Benaroya's gift was exactly what Charles Osborn had wanted. He had always seen the work of the Kreielsheimer Foundation — the acquisition of the land, the hiring of architects, the funding of studies — as the beginning, but knew it was the larger community that had to make it real. Mark Reddington, the project architect who worked with Osborn on the original design, agrees. "Charlie never imagined that Kreielsheimer would pay for a concert hall. He was trying to plant the seed in a way that would inspire others to get involved, and he was very persistent in that." On the day of the Benaroya gift announcement, Jack acknowledged his debt to Osborn: "Six or seven weeks ago, I was again reading about the Kreielsheimer Foundation's contributions of land and studies toward the concert-hall project. I thought somebody needed to give this a little impetus. That's when I called Gerry [Schwarz]."

That 1993 phone call to Schwarz, the Rainier Club lunch the next week, and the Benaroya commitment that followed, broke the dam. The Symphony mounted a record endowment and capital campaign leading to the realization, just five years later, of the concert hall dream. In less than half a year, from Mary Ann Champion's tearful December plea in Don Johnson's office to the Benaroya announcement in May, everything changed. The Concert Hall is in downtown Seattle, of course, and not at the site Charles Osborn had chosen. It is, rightfully, *Benaroya* Hall, but there's little doubt in the symphonic community that without Osborn's passion and dedication to the idea of the concert hall and without Don Johnson's support at a critical time, without the resources of the Kreielsheimer Foundation, there would be no hall. Birdwell: "Without Kreielsheimer, the idea would not have developed to the point where Jack would have come forward." Schwarz: "They're what kept it alive, kept it going, made it possible for us to dream — a dream that led to Jack's dream." Oboist John DeJarnatt: "Benaroya paid for the hall, but Kreielsheimer paid for the dream."

LMN architects' 1995 rendering of the new concert hall on the downtown site

On a side wall in the old Kreielsheimer Foundation offices there's a color photograph of Benaroya Hall. It's taken at dusk, so the inside of the lobby gives off a glow through the glass walls, shining like a lantern — an echo of the design Charles Osborn funded long ago for the Mercer Street site. On the margin Jerry Schwarz has written, to the Foundation, "thank you for helping us realize our dream." That dream, Benaroya Hall (and later McCaw Hall) are, for Don Johnson, "the greatest accomplishments" of the Foundation, even with the disappointment (for Don personally) of seeing the hall locate downtown, and even after some later difficulties with the Symphony administration over the Foundation's participation in the Concert Hall Capital Campaign. The concert hall is, he knows, the embodiment of Osborn's dream, of what Symphony musician John DeJarnatt calls Osborn's "grand gesture," the huge "leap of faith" that saved the Orchestra by boldly imagining a future. Would Osborn agree? Speight Jenkins is not alone in saying that Charlie would have fought to the end against a downtown site. "He bitterly resented the Art Museum going downtown. He would have had a conniption fit at the thought of the Symphony going downtown." DeJarnatt, though, believes that if "Charlie could come back and see this downtown site he would be able to step back and say to himself, 'that's O.K.' " We can't know, but the musical legacy of the Kreielsheimer Foundation is clear and enduring. "They owe them their homes (Benaroya Hall and McCaw Hall)," says *Times* critic Bargreen. The legacy is very *personal* as well. The trustees, Charles Osborn and Don Johnson, alone created the vision and made the choices for the Foundation. Johnson himself says, "If you disagree with what we did, the blame stops at the door of Osborn and Johnson." And the vision is *enormous*—in the new halls, in the programming, in the high artistic standards and expectations, and in the endowments that carry the Kreielsheimer legacy into the future.

In 1993, Deborah Card wrote the ultimate tribute to Osborn and Johnson and the Kreielsheimer Foundation in a small note just after the public announcement of Jack Benaroya's $15.8 million gift. She was writing about the concert hall, but her words speak as well to the new opera house, McCaw Hall, and to the enormous growth of the local arts community in the short life of the Foundation. She said, simply, "Thank you for being the catalyst for it all."

Seattle Opera

The Kreielsheimer Foundation's relationship with the Seattle Opera lacks the same drama, but it begins with Osborn and a 1984 phone call Opera General Director Speight Jenkins will never forget. He'd just finished performances of *The Ballad of Baby Doe*, his first opera with the company. The phone rang, "out of the blue," says Jenkins, with an irate Osborn on the other end of the line. "So far as I'm concerned," Osborn said, "your first opera was a bust. I didn't like the casting, I didn't like anything about it, and I want to improve your casting, and I don't know how to improve it except to give you more money to do it." Jenkins wasn't expecting the call, but he already knew about Osborn. "I'd heard he was a very crusty soul, and he was." Osborn was as good as his word, though, and committed to give Seattle Opera $100,000 a season to improve the singing cast, promising, "If I like the results, I'll keep it up." He did. So did his successor, Don Johnson, until the Foundation closed down in 2000. The annual distribution from a final Kreielsheimer endowment gift of $2 million will keep Osborn's $100,000 commitment to artistic quality at the Opera alive in perpetuity.

That yearly artistic commitment is only a fraction of Kreielsheimer's legacy at Seattle Opera, which Jenkins calls "an absolutely vital part of our success." It started with Osborn's phone call, but because the original

Kathy Magiera, managing director of the Seattle Opera during the 1990s

principal of the Foundation grew by a factor of five in the 1990s, Johnson's eight-year tenure as a co-trustee became far more influential. He gave away, in grant dollars, almost 85 percent of the Foundation's total worth. Johnson would say, in 2001, about that money growth, "We could dream, and we had the funding to do something about it." How they dreamed is as important as the dollars; the differing personalities of the two men profoundly shaped the work of the Kreielsheimer Foundation, and Seattle Opera.

Shortly after Osborn's death, Peter Donnelly, president of ArtsFund, then known as the Corporate Council for the Arts, invited Johnson to sit on the CCA Allocation Committee. "If you're going to be in charge of giving away this amount of money," he told Johnson, "you ought to know what's out there, and who's doing what." Johnson agreed, and both men say it gave the new Kreielsheimer trustee a tremendous crash course in the essentials of local arts organizations. Donnelly remembers Osborn as more of a loner, more aloof, but Johnson, he says, became a real part of the community. "There's a very rich and varied arts community here, and Don learned about that, Don nourished it, and Don got nourished by it." Kathy Magiera, the late managing director at Seattle Opera, recalled that Johnson's style, his almost daily engagement with the company, was apparent from the beginning. "With Don, I know that any time we asked him to attend anything, no matter how insignificant — even if it was a small event — he would be there. He took the time and effort to learn about the organization." That personal interest, and this was from the beginning a Foundation of *personal* interests, paid off in ways large and small.

Magiera remembers most fondly the 1993 *Norma* incident. A Seattle favorite, Carol Vaness, had signed to sing the demanding lead role in the Bellini opera, but she developed back problems and cancelled at the last minute. Desperate, Speight Jenkins broke one of his fundamental rules and

Left to right: Speight Jenkins, Mary Brazeau, and Jane Eaglen of the Seattle Opera, celebrating the June 2003 opening of McCaw Hall with Don and Dottie Johnson

brought in a singer he'd never heard, Jane Eaglen. The rest is operatic history. Jenkins says now, "I knew, after opening night, that I'd found the great Wagner singer of the era." Johnson and the Kreielsheimer Foundation had nothing to do with finding Eaglen, but in a December 1993 gesture long remembered at the company, Johnson, unsolicited, sent in $25,000 from the Foundation to cover the costs of bringing in Eaglen. He said, in a short note, "Please accept this Kreielsheimer Grant as a special and sincere vote of confidence in Speight Jenkins. You need to know your Seattle friends are not simply of the fair weather variety." Years after that small gift, Magiera would say, "It was out of the blue; we didn't ask him for additional funding. When you have someone at a foundation who says, 'I know this must be difficult and very trying for you,' it says quite a bit for that individual and the foundation." Jenkins says it happened because Don Johnson "paid attention, because he heard what was going on, and because he wanted to help."

Many other gifts and grants came to the Seattle Opera from the Kreielsheimer Foundation, including a crucial million-dollar gift (Jenkins calls it one of his "Big Four") to create a new production of Wagner's "Ring" in 2001. There was also a very personal gift of $50,000, in 2000, to boost the salary of Education Director Perry Lorenzo, whose pre-opera lectures Johnson found "not only intellectually rich, but entertaining."

Kreielsheimer Promenade at McCaw Hall

According to Magiera, "Don will not go to an opera without listening to Perry's talk first."

But the enduring Kreielsheimer opera legacy is in land and buildings, and in the funding to make them possible. Opera lovers walking the Kreielsheimer Promenade outside the new McCaw Hall will know that the Foundation gave the city $10 million to help fund the reconstruction. Across Mercer Street, the property Charles Osborn purchased for an art museum, and later held as the foundation of his concert hall vision, is now owned by Seattle Opera as the site of a new Opera Administrative Center. The Foundation gave the property and added a million-dollar challenge grant to help fund the project.

John Nesholm, the longtime president of the Opera Board and a close friend of Johnson, fits the Opera House gift into the long perspective of the Kreielsheimer Foundation. Just as Osborn's gift of land and persistence gave birth to the new symphony concert hall, he says, so did the Johnson Kreielsheimer gift give life to the new opera house campaign. Jenkins found the $10 million opera house grant all the more extraordinary for what it told him about the character of Don Johnson. After word of the lead Kreielsheimer gift went out, the McCaw family came in with a $20 million pledge for the hall, and with it wanted naming rights to the new building. Jenkins: "Most donors, in the situation in which Don found himself,

Entry lobby and interior of Kreielsheimer Promenade at McCaw Hall

would have said 'Get lost, I'm not going to give you a dime.' We were willing to forego the other gift, because we didn't want to hurt his feelings, but he wouldn't allow that. He saw the larger picture, and that was real statesmanship in terms of giving, and I will always be grateful. The man had a tremendous, big vision in order to do that."

Not counting the $10 million Opera House gift to the Seattle Center Foundation, which was given "for the benefit of the City of Seattle, Seattle Opera, and Pacific Northwest Ballet," the Kreielsheimer dollar impact on Seattle Opera approximates $11 million, more than the Foundation would give to any other arts organization. In Jenkins's time, when Seattle Opera built its international artistic reputation, four major givers made the difference: Michael Scott in the first eight years, then Patsy Collins, Marion McCaw Garrison, and Kreielsheimer. "Those four entities have given major, major money over the years I've been here," he says. "Without those four entities we would be a little 'B' or 'C' class opera company — a 'B' class opera company at best."

In 2000, the sunset year of the Kreielsheimer Foundation, John Nesholm, architect and Seattle Opera board president, wrote a note to Don

Johnson, praising him for the Foundation's work in the local arts community: "You have certainly maximized leverage in every project undertaken and have set an example that will be difficult to equal." For Nesholm, "leverage" is the key word in measuring the Kreielsheimer legacy. He meant, by leverage, using the resources of a foundation to create critical mass, to attract other funds, to turn a dream into reality. Osborn used the leverage of the Kreielsheimer Mercer Street block and the early architectural studies to keep the concert-hall idea afloat. Johnson used a $1 million endowment grant as leverage, as a green light for other donors, at a time when the survival of the Seattle Symphony was in question. He gave $10 million—leverage—to jump-start the Opera House renovation. ArtsFund's Peter Donnelly says the leverage of a grant at the right time sets a tone, challenges other donors, and gives legitimacy to fund-raising and capital campaigns that might otherwise wither. Johnson understood that power from the beginning. "Don understood the leverage he was bringing to the table," says Donnelly. "He didn't have to be heavy-handed. He knew it, and he knew that everyone knew it."

Other Musical Organizations

The Foundation used the same principle in reaching out to smaller musical organizations in the region. None of them received a fraction of the dollars that went to the Opera and the Symphony, but gifts from Kreielsheimer— conveying the approval of the Foundation—gave their work life as well as legitimacy with other donors.

Louise Kincaid, then executive director of the Northwest Chamber Orchestra, told the *Seattle Times*, in a 1997 interview, that challenge grants and support from the Kreielsheimer Foundation are "not only a leverage but also a stamp of approval in the donor community." Seven yearly Kreielsheimer gifts of $50,000 each in the 1990s allowed the Chamber Orchestra to grow artistically, to add more concerts, to build a wider donor base, to bring in more visible artists, and, most importantly, to become stable financially. In the daily life of an orchestra, a steady source of income is everything. With the Kreielsheimer money, says Kincaid, "we didn't have to sweat out each payroll. They've left us financially and artistically light-years ahead."

The Seattle Youth Symphony Orchestra was not a major recipient of Kreielsheimer grants, but a $25,000 gift in 1996, matching a Boeing grant, likely saved the Orchestra from collapse. Former Youth Symphony board President Lorrie Scott says that gift "was a tremendous boost for the morale of the organization," giving the board the confidence to raise new dollars in the community. "In my opinion," she wrote in a 2002 memo, "the money we received from Kreielsheimer and Boeing saved the organization."[†]

Just before the formal sunset of the Kreielsheimer Foundation, Johnson established a number of small endowments for the Chamber Orchestra, the Youth Symphony, the Seattle Chamber Music Festival, and the Bellevue Philharmonic. These gifts will provide steady operating funds in perpetuity. The dollars are always crucial in an arts community, but more important, for Chamber Music Festival Director Connie Cooper, is the climate change in fund-raising fostered by Kreielsheimer over its twenty-five years. Cooper says, "Kreielsheimer created a climate of giving in this community, a climate where art could thrive, and that benefited all of us."

[†] See the section on the Seattle Youth Symphony Orchestra in chapter 3 for further discussion of this group.

2 | Visual Arts
Sheila Farr

Creative Alliances

Walk into an art museum in Western Washington and you will likely spot the name Kreielsheimer somewhere on the wall. That's one obvious way of saying thank you for money that not only helped pay for the building, but prodded other benefactors to offer their support as well. Often a Kreielsheimer capital contribution was given in the form of a challenge grant, with trustee Don Johnson or his predecessor, Charles Osborn, working in the wings to ensure that the project would succeed.

Among the Northwest's prominent supporters of visual arts organizations, the Kreielsheimer Foundation has distributed nearly $38 million to museums, cultural institutions — such as the Alaska Native Heritage Center and Wing Luke Asian Museum in Seattle — and arts education. One of the primary benefactors of Kreielsheimer money was the Cornish College of the Arts, which received more than $11 million during the course of the Kreielsheimer Foundation, beginning with substantial scholarship grants from Osborn that were later made permanent by Johnson with the establishment of the Kreielsheimer Endowed Scholarship Fund in 2000. Osborn and Johnson both made substantial capital donations for expansion and renovation.

During the 1990s, just at the time National Endowment for the Arts funds began to be cut, the Kreielsheimer Foundation stepped up its giving to help keep regional museums growing. During that decade virtually every Western Washington art museum expanded and refurbished its facilities or began fund-raising for a new building. The Kreielsheimer Foundation supported the capital campaigns of the Seattle Art Museum (including renovation of the Asian Art Museum at Volunteer Park, the new downtown museum, and the Olympic Sculpture Park), the Museum of Northwest Art, the Tacoma Art Museum, the Bellevue Art Museum (since 2004 the Bellevue Arts Museum), and Tacoma's Museum of Glass. And that was just one facet of the Foundation's giving.

Why give so much to the visual arts?

Leo and Greye Kreielsheimer set the tone for the Foundation's gifts through their interest in painting. Although their collection wasn't extensive, they chose work by major Northwest artists to decorate their home, including Mark Tobey's 1930 watercolor *Hunchbacks*, and his 1934 painting *Shanghai*; Morris Graves's *Wood Pigeons* (1947); and an undated Kenneth Callahan oil called *Voyage Song*. They supported local museums through memberships and donations.

Trustee Johnson and his wife, Dorothy (Dottie), carried the Kreielsheimer torch with a passionate interest in the visual arts, and they remain active members of the arts community. Dottie, a potter, is a longtime volunteer at the Bellevue Arts Museum and a member of one of the museum guilds. Their daughter Karin, after receiving an architectural degree from the University of Washington, worked several years for glass artist Dale Chihuly. Johnson's mother, Edith Johnson, who received a Bachelor of Fine Arts degree in painting at the University of Washington, studied art there under an outstanding faculty, including Spencer Moseley, Alden Mason, Boyer Gonzales, Glen Alps, Robert Sperry, and George Tsutakawa, who remained one of her favorite Northwest artists. Don, who describes himself as "a frustrated architect," inherited his mother's admiration for the Tsutakawa family, all of whom are active in the regional art scene.

"The Tsutakawas' art — father and son — was always something my wife and I liked," Johnson says, referring to Gerard, who carries on his father's work as a sculptor. "My mother greatly admired George Tsutakawa, and when she studied with him at UW he would take the class on Saturday field trips, bringing his children. It was above and beyond what professors were expected to do." Johnson recalls that one of the last things his mother told him before she died at age ninety-two was how much she had learned from George Tsutakawa.

The Johnsons' personal art collection includes work by both George and Gerry Tsutakawa, as well as James Washington Jr., Doris Chase, Joseph Goldberg, Kenneth Callahan, Morris Graves, and Dale Chihuly. Johnson readily admits that he has shown a strong commitment to supporting work by Northwest artists in his grant-giving for the Foundation.

By his desk at the Kreielsheimer offices, Johnson keeps a "Peanuts" comic strip. In the first frame, Charlie Brown, looking noble, declares to Lucy: "When I grow up, I want to be a great philanthropist." Lucy — always the wet blanket — puts him in his place with the retort: "To be a philanthropist, you have to be rich." Charlie Brown digests that information, then replies, "I want to be a great philanthropist with someone else's money."

If that was Johnson's motto, from all indications he has been a success. Many recipients of Kreielsheimer visual arts grants mention the sense of responsibility Johnson brought to the task of administering the Foundation's money. "In meeting with Don from the very beginning, he talked about who else could be brought to the table," said Diane Douglas, director of the Bellevue Art Museum during the years of its capital campaign and expansion project. "He was in from the start and understood the leverage that the Foundation could bring. It was very strategically done."

As most fledgling philanthropists quickly discover, giving away piles of money may sound like great fun, but in fact, to be effective, it requires a lot of homework and diligence. Gleaning the most appropriate recipients out of a sea of voracious organizations is no easy job. Former BAM director Douglas describes herself as one of "the sharks in the water" that came to the Kreielsheimer Foundation in search of funding. She remembers Johnson's attitude toward his job. "I think he wore that mantle in the beginning very uncomfortably," she says. "He really felt the gravity of what he was doing."

Henry Art Gallery Director Richard Andrews concurs, describing Johnson's methods as thorough and involved. As a fund-raiser, Andrews says he's grateful that the Northwest is beginning to foster private foundations like Kreielsheimer and the Allen Foundation for the Arts that can step forward as examples to the community. "They're taking an ecological approach. You need diversity; you need variety; you need the big institutions and the fledgling groups. You need to take some risks," he says. It's important to remember that the Kreielsheimer Foundation predates Microsoft and the Seattle area's generation of high-tech wealth, and that the Foundation's period of greatest giving came at a time of government cutbacks to the National Endowment for the Arts.

"The Kreielsheimer Foundation has been a very generous and reliable source for capital projects at exactly the time this community needed to build its facilities up," Andrews says. "So to have a Foundation emerge at the greatest time of need has been catalytic." Johnson's choices for Kreielsheimer grants tended toward building and endowment gifts, and those, Andrews points out, are ones that keep growing and continue to pay off over time. A total of $1,539,940 was given to the Henry Art Gallery for these purposes.

For a small, emerging museum like La Conner's Museum of Northwest Art (MONA), Kreielsheimer support was pivotal. "They came in early in our capital campaign," says Director Susan Parke. "At that time nobody was paying a lot of attention to Northwest art. I think it helped validate our purpose." She says Johnson believed in the importance of regional art and helped rally support with a stringent challenge grant. "I think of it as a local project that needed substantial Seattle help," Johnson recalls. "We offered a $75,000 capital grant. Jack Benaroya said, 'Don, I'll match you.' He wanted to give to a museum that promised to show Northwest art." Johnson has followed MONA's progress with interest and says he wants to see that the museum gets accredited by the American Association of Museums, a process which will require substantial funding to install sophisticated climate-control systems and other improvements in the facility. The Kreielsheimer and Benaroya grants energized the capital campaign and it went on to reach its goal and to enable the museum to construct its new facility.

Working on behalf of a private foundation, Johnson had total control, within the guidelines that Leo Kreielsheimer set down in his will, to bestow money the way he saw fit. He made his choices based on personal taste as well as a lot of homework. "My wife loves visual art; I love visual art. My firm, Bogle & Gates, had a fine collection," he says. "I have enough confidence in my own taste." But Johnson says there is an additional element as well. "I'm a great believer in good networking, getting the opinions and comments of people in the community who really know about a subject. You talk to people like Virginia Wright or Marshall Hatch, to Don Foster and John Braseth — people in the business. You talk to Gerry Tsutakawa or good collectors like the Benaroyas . . . I felt that an important element of

Left to right: Ayume Tsutakawa, George Tsutakawa, and Charles F. Osborn at the 1989 dedication of Tsutakawa's *Centennial Fountain* on the Seattle University campus

giving Kreielsheimer money was to get a result that was appreciated by a significant number in the community.

For Johnson, the perfect example is the George Tsutakawa's *Centennial Fountain* at the heart of the Seattle University campus on First Hill, installed during Osborn's tenure at the Kreielsheimer helm. The work, dedicated in 1989, is one of Tsutakawa's last and finest, a convergence of steel and spraying water that soothes and dazzles. Surrounded by a quiet arrangement of stones and plantings, the fountain and its plaza anchor the campus as a place of rest and gathering for the students. Tsutakawa grew up in the neighborhood and used to walk the campus. He told his son, Gerry, he believed that the *Centennial Fountain* would be one of his most important works.

Johnson later stepped in with Kreielsheimer assistance when the downtown Seattle Public Library moved out of its old building in preparation for the construction of a new facility designed by Rem Koolhaas. That meant that the fate of Tsutakawa's *Fountain of Wisdom*, beautifully sited on the Fifth Avenue plaza, was uncertain. "I was concerned that the beautiful fountain on Fifth Avenue would get put away and forgotten about in the new construction," Johnson said. "I gave the grant on the condition that the funds be expended as necessary to underwrite costs for temporary removal and reinstallation of the fountain at the new library." The fountain was installed in May 2004 at the Fourth Avenue and Madison corner of the new library building, where it will become part of the exterior landscape.

The Kreielsheimer Money at Work

One of Johnson's last grant decisions before the Kreielsheimer Foundation completed its mission in 2000 was a pledge of $1 million to the Washington Art Consortium. The Consortium was founded in 1973 by art collector Virginia Wright and remains a national example of an innovative approach to institutional collecting.

With money from the Virginia Wright Fund and the National Endowment for the Arts, a group of smaller museums and universities were able to join forces to acquire two outstanding groups of images: one of works on paper, the other of photographs. The artworks rotate for exhibit among the member museums, which include the Western Gallery at Western Washington University; the Whatcom County Museum in Bellingham; the Northwest Museum of Arts and Culture (formerly the Cheney Cowles Memorial State Museum) in Spokane; the Tacoma Art Museum; and the Museum of Art at Washington State University, Pullman. The Seattle Art Museum, which Wright says has always held an advisory role in the Consortium, is now a full member of the group.

While the purpose of the collection was initially to acquire works by top-name twentieth-century artists, most based in New York, the Consortium is now committed to Northwest regional art as well—but not through purchases, Wright says. "I think the Consortium with its own staff can do a lot to promote Northwest art, possibly with publications, with programming, but it [the collection] shouldn't grow indefinitely." Wright believes it will be better if collectors give works to individual members of the Consortium, which have facilities to store and care for the work.

With income from the Kreielsheimer endowment, members of the Consortium are now in the process of strengthening its staff. The plan is to create a database of the Northwest art holdings of member institutions, which Wright estimates at some 4,000 pieces. "That will be a fantastic tool for curators and scholars of the future, to help them put together exhibitions of Northwest art." The Wrights committed to give a matching endowment gift of $1 million to the Consortium within the next few years.

One condition of the Kreielsheimer grant, stipulated by Johnson, was that the Consortium become a nonprofit organization. That means it will be able to apply for grants to help with conservation costs and maintenance of the collection. "That was good vision on Don's part," Wright says, and notes that "It is typical of his attention to business details when bestowing Kreielsheimer funds."

In a letter to Don Johnson dated October 7, 2004, Washington Art Consortium President Chris Bruce reviews the members' commitment, both to documenting the extent of Northwest art in their several collections and to collaborating on projects that feature it. The president's summary concludes with a reiteration of thanks for "the generosity of the Kreielsheimer Foundation in supporting the WAC's deep commitment to the art of our region."

A Personal Style of Giving

When evaluating grant applicants, Don Johnson notes that you can't just blurt out "Hey, this is perfect!" the moment someone asks you for money. But when he was first approached for a donation to the Seattle Art Museum's downtown Olympic Sculpture Park — proposed for a strip of waterfront near Myrtle Edwards Park — that's exactly what went through his mind. "I grew up in this community and there's no place left for a sculpture garden with a setting like this," Johnson said. "I decided right there I'd give a million up front if it was properly organized. It's one of the most exciting projects, in my mind, a total no-brainer."

Virginia Wright, a trustee of SAM and one of the prime forces behind the sculpture park plan, was impressed with Johnson's foresight. "He got it right away," she recalled. "He saw what a great project it was right off the bat. A lot of people didn't."

Wright said that the size of the project and the fact that the Sculpture Park would be located away from the museum's main facility made some board members skeptical. "In a way it is a very idealistic thing for the museum to be doing. We're providing a public park for Seattle," Wright said, noting that the Sculpture Park grounds will be open to the public free of charge and provide much-needed green space and waterfront access for downtown. "Don was right there." And as anyone who has tried to raise money for a nonprofit organization knows, having a well-known name, like Kreielsheimer, on the donor list makes the project an easier sell to other benefactors. Wright mentioned that Bill Gates, Sr., head of one of the world's richest philanthropic organizations, had recently pointed out to her that fund-raising is all about what the other guy is doing. "If certain people get involved early on, others follow," Wright said.

"The Kreielsheimer Foundation's generous financial support has impacted SAM in so many ways," said Mimi Gardner Gates, Seattle Art Museum director. "They have helped to ensure the growth and stability of the museum with support ranging from our endowment to exhibition spaces, the future Olympic Sculpture Park, and much, much more. Their generosity will leave a meaningful legacy for future generations of Seattleites."

The flexibility and personal involvement of Kreielsheimer Foundation giving made it a boon to big institutions like the Seattle Art Museum, but not necessarily an ideal fit for less-established organizations such as Artist Trust, founded in 1986 to support and encourage artists in Washington State through individual grants. The Kreielsheimer Foundation tended to be conservative in its grant-giving, focusing its major gifts on established institutions: the top twenty-one recipients on the Kreielsheimer list ended up with about ninety percent of the total funds. In disbursing those funds, Osborn and Johnson did not rely on a formal application process. Grant recipients were selected through the research and preferences of its administrators and their network of advisors, which in later years included information and resources provided by the Corporate Council for the Arts/ArtsFund.

Executive Director Barbara Courtney describes Artist Trust's relationship with the Kreielsheimer Foundation as "a long and interesting courtship." "When I came [to Artist Trust]," Courtney said, "we'd been sending letters to Don Johnson and asking to meet with him and submit a full grant proposal." As the Kreielsheimer Foundation drew near its 2000 closing deadline, it made a challenge endowment grant of $150,000 to Artist Trust, to be held by the Kreielsheimer Remainder Foundation.

Would Courtney have preferred an outright gift? "Sure, absolutely," she says. Seattle attorney Jim Tune, vice president and secretary of the Kreielsheimer Remainder Foundation (KRF), says he understands Courtney's point of view, but defends Johnson's reasons for placing the grant in the KRF. "Its sole purpose is to take custody of the funds, to invest, and to distribute the funds to the named beneficiaries," Tune said. "I think Don wanted to be absolutely sure all those funds remain as real endowment."

Most of the money in KRF is allocated to smaller organizations such as On the Boards, Artist Trust, and the Northwest Chamber Orchestra. Tune said that Johnson's perspective as a lawyer made him extra cautious about the possible failure of such groups. "These are very small organizations and it's not clear they've arrived at the institutional state where they will continue to survive," Tune said. He noted that if one of the groups were to fold, there are provisions that would disburse the endowment money among the others. "Say hypothetically that On The Boards were to fold — it's gone through tremendous difficulties with the board — if it had custody of the endowment funds and went into bankruptcy, that money would be used up." By strictly regulating the way the endowment funds are held, Johnson insured that the Kreielsheimer money would be available to benefit other surviving organizations.

Despite her philosophical differences with the Kreielsheimer's approach, Courtney praises the example of giving that the Foundation set. Like many others in the Northwest, she feels concerned about the region's philanthropic future. "Here during our generation, during the '80s and '90s, the Kreielsheimer Foundation was a centerpiece of giving in the art community — but in ten years, mention the name and people will say 'Who is that?' Hopefully somebody else will step in. There's the Allen Foundation for the Arts, but who else? This story could be a good example."

That's exactly what trustee Don Johnson is hoping to do: to provide insight into the difficulties of philanthropic giving and inspiration as to its rewards. "It was interesting," he said, thinking back on his stewardship of the Kreielsheimer Foundation. "There's a lot of stress to it: You worry, 'Am I wasting this money?' One of the gratifying things was the high caliber of support that volunteers in the arts provided . . . You're dealing with some really nice people, dedicated people. It's been fun."

Theatre

3

Jean Sherrard

Seattle Repertory Theatre

Any history of the theater in Seattle must begin with the 1962 World's Fair. Before then, there were only two professional arts organizations in Seattle — the Seattle Symphony Orchestra and the Seattle Art Museum. Afterward, flush with cash and a surfeit of buildings in the newly constructed Seattle Center, the city encouraged and supported the Science Center, the Opera, and the spanking new Seattle Repertory Theatre. In its first season, the Rep catapulted into the first rank of regional theaters with an unheard-of 12,000 subscribers. As the first professional Seattle theater, its mission was a traditional one: that of presenting established drama ranging from Shakespeare to Shaw, from Chekhov to Arthur Miller. And while that mission has changed with the times, increasing in range and scope, the preeminence of the Rep has continued.

Peter Donnelly remembers the early years as thrilling but challenging. Running the young theater demanded the skills of a military planner. "Our scene shop moved around the city; it was in Ballard part of the time, in North Lake Union part of the time, and occasionally south of Pioneer Square; our wardrobe was at the top of the playhouse; we operated in the playhouse; our administration was in the Food Circus building; our box office was next door where Pacific Northwest Ballet is today; our second theater was downtown under the Monorail, and then moved to what became the Convention Center . . . nearly twenty-five percent of our resources were being spent on logistics." Everything changed in 1983 with the opening of the Bagley Wright Theatre. Seven locations were brought under one roof. Now the Rep was free to focus on "mature artistic aspirations."

Under then-Artistic Director Daniel Sullivan, new play development thrived. The new mainstage was the near-fulfillment of a dream. But the dream had a second act. Managing Director Benjamin Moore recalls: "When I arrived in '85, the first and foremost thing on Dan Sullivan's mind was building a small theater." While the Poncho Forum had served as a second performance space since the opening of the Bagley Wright, its small size, limited seating, and boxy, multiuse design made it less than ideal. A dedicated second stage was needed in which to mount smaller-scale and experimental works that would not suit an 800-seat mainstage. It would also attract an audience looking for a more intimate theater experience.

By the early '90s, Sullivan and Moore were preparing a pitch to the Kreielsheimer Foundation. And just to be sure, they stacked the deck. "The truth is, they sandbagged me," Don Johnson recalls with a chuckle. "It was supposed to be an informal get-together with five or six people, and when I showed up, there are more than a dozen, one of whom was Wendy Wasserstein." Ben Moore recalls, "That was when I think we got his attention in a very real way. I've always felt that Don had this experience of stepping from one world into another that he never expected to have much to do with. He came to really relish his exposure to the arts."

Don had retired from the Bogle & Gates law firm soon after assuming his trustee obligations to the Kreielsheimer Foundation. It was only natural for him to bring a corporate lawyer's keen sense of long-term strategy and leverage. In trying to balance present and future needs, Don was convinced that major capital campaigns should be tied to endowment creation. Peter Donnelly explains, "For an established arts organization, there are four important building blocks: balancing the annual operating budget, building cash reserves, completing the physical plant, and then funding an endowment." Don thought it propitious to move the last two building blocks into place simultaneously. "I remember going to Don to ask him for support to build the Leo K," recalls Benjamin Moore with a chuckle. "Immediately, he began talking endowment. There I was, trying to reintroduce our concept and our thinking, trying to get bricks-and-mortar money out of the Kreielsheimer Foundation, but Don would only give it to us with the express condition that we set up our own foundation. And anything we didn't use of capital money to build the theater would go into the endowment. Miracle of miracles, this actually happened. We completed the Leo K on time and under budget and plowed what was left over into the Seattle Rep Foundation."

Don's involvement with the Rep grew along with the new theater. He paid careful attention to every aspect of its construction, from the blueprints to the finished building. Jim Tune, who was his partner at Bogle & Gates, describes him as "endlessly meticulous," while Benjamin Moore marvels at Don's "legendary attention to detail." As the new theater approached completion, Moore and Johnson met repeatedly to discuss many of the details, from the exterior color of the building to what name the theater should be given.

Having initially proposed that the Kreielsheimer support should be in the form of a naming grant, Moore had a bit of a problem. The name "Kreielsheimer" was hard to pronounce. Was it "Krells-heimer," "Krell-sheimer," "Krayal-sheimer," or "Krayals-heimer"? After years of familiarity, even the staff at the Rep had trouble getting it right. How could the average theatergoer ever manage it? Besides, the Kreielsheimer name was popping up all over town, which could lead to all kinds of confusion. That was when Moore had a great notion: The Leo K It had snap and rhythm. What's more, it was easy to remember. But how would Don Johnson react? He needn't have worried. "Don got a big kick out of this," recalls Moore. "He and Leo went way back and he thought Leo would have loved it. Now it's become fully and inalterably imprinted on this institution."

At the Leo K. Theatre dedication, Don had a pleasant surprise in store. Wendy Wasserstein stepped out from the wings and recalled their first meeting. "About three years ago, Ben Moore called me and said, 'You have got to come to Seattle and meet Don Johnson.' 'Don Johnson!' I said. 'He's in Miami.' " When the laughter died down, she praised the "jewel box of a theater" in which she was standing, and the vital role that the Kreielsheimer Foundation had played in making the dream a reality.

The Seattle Repertory Theatre Foundation, with a substantial injection of funds for the under-budget Leo K, was off to a solid start. Don Johnson was eager to build and consolidate the endowment. When Dan Sullivan decided to leave the Rep, the Kreielsheimer Foundation memorialized him with a million-dollar contribution to the endowment. "This really propelled us into the notion of actually beginning an endowment campaign," says Moore, "which came into play much sooner than I had ever imagined it could."

Another milestone in the Kreielsheimer legacy at the Rep all began on a California beach. Rep Artistic Director Sharon Ott was working as a guest director with a theater in San Jose. Don and his wife, Dottie, invited her to their second home in Carmel for an overnight visit and a chat. Don and Dottie took Sharon to Point Lobos for a picnic. The weather was glorious, Don remembers, and they relaxed on the beach for nearly three hours. Sharon spoke of her love of Shakespeare and his importance to theater, language, and culture. Given its facilities and resources, the Rep was particularly well-positioned to commit to an annual Shakespeare production—a Shakespeare cycle even. "This is where Don got really engaged," says Ben Moore. "He saw in our ambitions something that reminded him of what Speight Jenkins was doing with the Ring."

Ott had planted a seed that day, one that grew over the next couple of years into the "Shakespeare Initiative," to be funded over four years to the tune of $1 million by the Kreielsheimer Foundation. True to form, Don encouraged the Rep to use this funding to leverage more funding. Ben Moore recalls: "On the one hand, he crafted an intricate scheme to foster this initiative, while on the other hand creating an opportunity for us to encourage other support." In 2000, the Kreielsheimer Foundation gave another $1 million in support of the Signature Works Fund, meant to overlap and complement the Shakespeare Initiative. To date, the Rep Foundation has raised nearly two-thirds of a hoped-for $15 million endowment. "We're never going to be able to do everything we want to do," reflects Ben Moore, "and the limitations and the restraints are as much a part of creative process as anything else. But the truth is that without the endowment we're hard-pressed to address some of our critical needs." Don's mix of cautious attention to detail and audacious vision for the future propelled the Rep much faster—and further—than it had expected into a graceful and secure middle age.

Book-It Repertory Theatre

While the Kreielsheimer Foundation was dedicated to fortifying and improving the prospects of major art institutions, equally effective grant-making was being done on a much smaller scale. The Book-It Repertory Theatre is a case in point. Dedicated to adapting works of literature in a "reader's theater" style, with dialogue and narrative intact, Book-It was cooked up in Jane Jones's kitchen in New York City in 1986. Encouraged by Ben Moore (her former teacher from the American Theatre Conservatory in San Francisco), she relocated to Seattle and joined a small collective of local theater artists, where her evolving ideas were eagerly adopted. Long story short: Years of operating on a shoestring with some spectacular successes. Small touring productions and commissioned works had evolved into working partnerships with major theaters and talented, often well-known actors like Tom Hulce and Linda Hunt. Jane and her co-artistic director Myra Platt worked hard to ensure that Book-It thrived creatively, but each season ended with a cliffhanger. How would they pay their bills? All small theaters expect to live month-to-month, week-to-week, day-by-day; it's a part of the creative process—and yet the struggle for survival takes its toll. Building up enough of a reserve to weather the lean times is every young theater's goal, and one that had thus far eluded Book-It.

One October evening in 1996, Don and Dottie Johnson went to a premiere of *Lady Chatterley's Lover* at Book-It's tatty but comfortable digs on Westlake Avenue. Ann Ramsay-Jenkins, then-president of the Seattle Rep board of directors, had encouraged them to attend. A staunch supporter since the Book-It/Rep coproduction of John Irving's *Cider House Rules*, Ramsay-Jenkins had hopes that, with a bit more exposure, Don Johnson would also become a fan. Jane Jones and Myra Platt recall their own nervousness at the time: "Don and Dottie walked up those old steps into this tiny funky space seating fifty people, and we thought, What *could* they be thinking? Not that it didn't have charm, but it was like the secret den of a secret society. And yet after the seeing the quality of that show, Don understood the potential of Book-It."

Right off the bat, Don suggested that Book-It mount a tour through Kreielsheimer Foundation–supported venues throughout Washington State. Jane and Myra, then unpaid, were working at capacity; from writing, acting, directing, and managing Book-It, to doing the janitorial work. They knew they couldn't even consider touring until they found—and funded—a managing director, but it all seemed highly unlikely. Unbeknownst to Jane and Myra, however, Ann Ramsay-Jenkins was hatching a plan of her own. She collared Don at the Foundation offices. "I know you're not crazy about endowing a position," she told him, "but we could think about a multiple-year grant for managing director that would allow these girls to focus entirely on the artistic side." Don told her to write it up.

A few weeks later, right around Christmas, Ann Ramsay-Jenkins threw a fund-raiser for Book-It, but it was more accurately a surprise party. John

Irving was in town and had agreed to read from *Owen Meany*. Rounding out an invited guest list of movers and shakers were Bill and Melinda Gates, just returned from China. Don Johnson, though he declined to take part in "any kind of shenanigans" (Ann Ramsay-Jenkins's phrase), was there to supply the evening's flourish of high drama.

After John Irving finished his reading, Ann joined him at the front of the room, carrying a fancy box with bows and ribbons and a red Santa hat. From out of the hat, she pulled a red Rudolph nose and put it on Irving, then she donned the hat. Gleefully, she relates what happened next: " 'Myra and Jane,' I said, 'I'd like you to come up here. I have a Christmas present for you.' So they come up and unwrap the box, and inside there's a cardboard *K* that I made, covered in glitter with a ribbon attached so you can hang it around your neck. So they're holding this up and I ask, 'What does this remind you of? What do you think the *K* stands for? I'll give you a clue — it's not a cereal and it's not a strike and it's not Santa Klaus . . .' And at first they just can't figure it out, and then Myra says, 'Kreiel . . .' and puts her hand over her mouth. And I said, 'What? Say that louder.' And she says, 'Kreielsheimer?' — and then she and Jane fell apart in the best way, crying and jumping up and down."

Don stood up and delivered a short speech praising Book-It's extraordinary artistry and the relevance and importance of great literature. Then he presented them with a check for $45,000, the first installment of a five-year grant. "It was a huge deal," recalls Myra Platt, "the biggest grant Book-It had ever gotten. Not just a stamp of approval, but a stepping stone to financial stability." Yet Don's involvement didn't end there. For the next several years, Don wrote letters and made phone calls encouraging larger theaters to let Book-It use their off-season stages. "It was all Don's idea," says Jane Jones. "We had management and artistic directors call and tell us, 'Now you be sure and let Don Johnson know we said yes to your performing in our venue.' " Myra and Jane share a glance and grin. They've each been finishing the other's sentences for years, occasionally correcting and backfilling. Now they're right in synch. Jane concludes: "It was suddenly as if Book-It had a dad, because Don didn't just make the grant and walk away; he helped advise us as well." "Like a dad," Myra repeats. "It really felt like a personal investment on his part."

Kreielsheimer Foundation support of the Intiman Theatre was somewhat muted until Don Johnson's tenure began in the early '90s. But as far as Managing Director Laura Penn is concerned that wasn't necessarily a negative. "Before the mid-nineties, I don't think we were ready for the rigor that Don required. We were brought into the circle at just the right time for us — which, fortuitously, was when Kreielsheimer was ready to offer support." And when that support came, it was substantial.

Intiman, founded by Megs Booker in 1972, had grown from a sixty-five-seat "broom-closet of a theater" with an annual budget of several thousand dollars to a regional theatrical powerhouse with an operating budget in the millions. Before moving into a beautifully renovated Seattle Center Playhouse, Intiman had, like so many other theaters, lived the gypsy life, wandering the city in search of spaces in which to perform. It's the sort of life that fosters the can-do, make-do approach by which theater professionals have learned to thrive. The Playhouse itself was lacking a convenient rehearsal space, and rather than building its own Intiman was contemplating off-site leasing. Managing Director Laura Penn recalls, "At the time, there were a bazillion capital campaigns around town and we were a little reluctant to join the crowd." Then the Kreielsheimer Foundation stepped in.

While the Intiman didn't have the capital needs of ACT or the Rep, they had embarked on an upgrade program with a comparatively modest budget of $2 million. Don had already committed $250,000 to that campaign, but he felt that the renovation as planned was incomplete. "They desperately needed the space, but had decided they couldn't afford it." Laura Penn recalls Don's matter-of-fact attitude. " 'You need a rehearsal hall,' he said, 'So build one.' We went 'Whoa!' — but that's what convinced us to jump back into the campaign."

"The Intiman Theatre had a fine bunch of people on their board: Pam Schell, Ida Cole, Susan Potts, Mark Kittner. And I made them a challenge," said Don, "If they would build the rehearsal hall they needed, I'd raise their capital grant to half a million." "Intiman's always been on the modest side," reflects Penn, "but Don encouraged us to be a little bolder. And he was completely right. Without his encouragement we wouldn't have taken that further step. Of course, Kreielsheimer didn't pay for the space all by itself, but the additional money helped enormously, not only in leveraging other funds, but also by giving us a real shot in the arm." Intiman named the rehearsal hall the Greye Kreielsheimer Rehearsal Hall in appreciation for the Foundation's special efforts.

As he had with many other major arts organizations, Don pushed hard for an Intiman endowment campaign. His view of endowments as essential institutional building blocks had already altered the arts landscape in the Northwest. And this was no idle opinion. As Laura Penn quips, "He put the Foundation's money where his mouth is." Don got the ball rolling with a million-dollar challenge gift to set up the foundation. An Intiman board member had already pledged a million in matching funds. Penn recalls strolling over to the nearby Kreielsheimer Foundation offices with the Intiman's board president and the president of the newly minted Intiman Foundation in tow.

Don had suggested that the Intiman set up a separate board to manage its endowment, and while that was not a condition of the grant Penn discovered it was excellent advice. "Don does not like organizations managing their operations and endowments together with the same board. He wants those moneys separate . . . and there are some real advantages. It's a place for past trustees to go; it's just a little more businesslike. They have their separate Board of Directors, their separate 501(c)3, and that's where the money is managed." Don and Jim Tune had spent many long hours drawing up the Intiman paperwork. He laid out final copies on the table. After the necessary signatures were affixed, Penn recalls, "Don asked, cool as a cucumber, 'Would you like some more?' I stuttered and stumbled — it took me completely by surprise. But we said, 'Uh, sure.' Out of the blue, Don said, 'We'd like to give you another million dollars for the endowment.' I just about fell off my chair. It was beautiful."

It is axiomatic that theater, compared to the other performing arts (ballet, opera, the symphony), is undercapitalized. Often theaters are last in line with the begging cup, or as Penn puts it, "at the bottom rung of the totem pole." She would argue that the Kreielsheimer Foundation's encouragement of endowment creation among local "major" theaters was timely and propitious. Don took advantage of a booming economy to foster and support multiple endowments whose creation may otherwise have been delayed by years or even decades. Peter Donnelly takes the long view: "It isn't something you announce on Tuesday and do on Thursday. An endowment is a state of mind as much as a project. You start using your endowment after a fairly short period of time — as soon as you've got enough in it to start generating some money. The rule of thumb is that you use five percent of the net worth."

What happens during an economic downturn? "An organization that started an endowment drive ten years ago doesn't stop the drive when the economy goes bad. The endowment is still there — you just may not be getting the same level of contributions, but it's always there, it's always being added to; people are dying and leaving money to it. Once you've got it in place it grows; or it's supposed to — if you're lucky it grows."

Empty Space Theatre

In the fall of 1992, Melissa Hines, managing director of the Empty Space Theatre, was considering her options. At best, they were bleak indeed. The Space, after nearly twenty-five years of consistently presenting some of the most cutting-edge theater in Seattle, was threatened with extinction. Not that it came as any surprise. A move from their scruffy digs on Capital Hill to tony Merrill Place in Pioneer Square in the mid-'80s had gone badly from the start. The innovative private/public partnership that gave the Space the capital to build a state-of-the-art midsized theater, saddled them with an eighteen-percent interest rate on a million-dollar debt, as well as a rent that had been arbitrarily doubled to nearly five dollars per square foot. After that move, for the first time in its history, the Empty Space had run up a deficit.

"Even though we were rebuilding audience in the new location," remembers Hines, "rebuilding our budget, doing all the appropriate things — we were cash-strapped the entire time without a safety net." Over almost five years struggling to survive at Merrill Place, the financial situation went from bad to worse, until, in a negotiated departure agreement, The Space walked away from the building and the debt, and moved into the old Pioneer Square Theatre. Hines spent the next three years, from 1989 to 1992, trying to get the theater back on its feet. "Put it this way: we were back to square one. We had eliminated our deficit and pulled ourselves together again. But there was a sort of dreariness about the situation; we could not get the subscribers to come down. It's hard to do risk-taking work on stage when your audience is worried about their car being broken into in the parking lot."

Kurt Beattie, then artistic director, had assembled three groundbreaking seasons, but the audiences never materialized. By October 1992, Hines knew the Space was at a critical juncture—and the choices were clear-cut. "Either we should go forward wholeheartedly, or minimize the damage and the losses at the point where we could." The entire staff voluntarily went off salary, the utilities were turned off, and season subscribers were asked for a six-week grace period during which the money from their subscriptions would be put in escrow (or if they preferred, they could request a refund). "Only one or two took a refund, bless their hearts," recalls Hines.

During that hiatus, the Empty Space board met and discussed possible courses of action, from filing for Chapter 11 to moving to a space that had opened up in Fremont. That was when Don Johnson, newly installed co-trustee of the Kreielsheimer Foundation, saw a letter published in the *Seattle Times* on November 8, 1992. Written by playwright, fisherman, and longtime supporter of the Empty Space Don Downing of Indianola, the letter to the editor detailed the troubles of "a unique Seattle institution," and lamented its potential loss. In conclusion, Downing wrote: "Are there no philanthropists in the Seattle area who recognize the importance of wholeheartedly supporting one of the Pacific Northwest's great theatres?" The response to that heartfelt plea came sooner than anyone could have expected.

The following day, Don Johnson walked into the office of Elaine Spencer, his partner at Bogle & Gates and an Empty Space board member, set the article on her desk, and asked if it were true. Would the Space close its doors forever "for want of a lousy $95,000?" Spencer was only too happy to give him a quick review of the situation. With quiet amusement, Johnson recalls his response: "What if I gave you a two-to-one challenge grant—say, $31,667, one-third of the total—could you raise the rest by the end of the year and secure the Fremont Palace?" "I'll find out," Spencer replied. The moment Don left her office, she picked up the phone and called Melissa Hines. Jim Tune, a partner at Bogle & Gates and board president of the Seattle Repertory Theatre, lauds Spencer's determination and commitment. "Elaine made sure Don understood how perilous the situation was at Empty Space."

Don Johnson had only recently assumed his responsibilities at the Kreielsheimer Foundation following the recent death of its first trustee Charles Osborn. In 1985, the Foundation had given the Empty Space a generous grant of $100,000 to support their move into Merrill Place. The next year, Hines requested another grant to help stabilize the theater. Osborn offered $50,000 for program support, but he had added a caveat. "The message we got was, here is one bridge gift," says Hines. "Don't come back to us again until you are a stable organization with a sound balance sheet. I heard that message."

Under Don Johnson, the Kreielsheimer message had changed, as Hines was delighted to discover. "Luck sent us the very person I wouldn't have approached," she recalls. "Don interested himself in us and took a risk. He was our angel." The challenge grant helped the Empty Space raise the matching dollars and move to Fremont. "If Don Johnson hadn't stepped up, we might have chosen to close the organization . . . it was an extraordinary gesture on his part."

For a time, the Empty Space flourished in their new digs in Fremont. The Kreielsheimer Foundation had played a major role in stabilizing the revitalized, midsized theater throughout the '90s. "From artistic objectives to physical infrastructure, we achieved our goals on every front. Don was always refreshingly willing to talk about the large things, about complex goals. And that is truly rare."

In the new millennium, disaster struck on two fronts, local and national. The 2001 earthquake that rocked Seattle on February 28 also destabilized the Space's Fremont aging brick building, causing extensive damage. While insurance covered major repairs, the offices and productions had to be temporarily relocated, resulting in unexpected debt. After September 11 and a plunging economy, the Empty Space found, as did many arts groups across the country, that the well of private and public giving had run dry. By October 2004, the theater found itself more than $300,000 in debt.

As before, the community rallied round the Space, raising, largely through small donations, more than $400,000 by January 31, 2005. At press time, the future of the Empty Space Theatre, while by no means secure, shows definite signs of revitalization. The Space and Seattle University have agreed that the Space will move out of Fremont and perform its 2006–7 season at Seattle University. This agreement also provides for an interchange between Space staff and actors and Seattle University students.

Seattle Children's Theatre

In its formative years, the Seattle Children's Theatre (SCT) got no respect, laments Artistic Director Linda Hartzell. Back then, "it wasn't cool to care about a theater for young audiences . . . Don Johnson was one of the first people that cared about the Children's Theatre and showed interest in us before we had grown up a little bit."

SCT has had to live by a different set of rules from the beginning. The average theater needs to reach seventy-percent capacity over a four- or five-week run to break even, while the Children's Theatre budgets for ninety-percent capacity over an eight- to fourteen-week run. In addition, ticket prices average two-thirds less than those at similarly sized theaters for adults, while artists' salaries remain comparable. "It means we have to work three times harder for the same amount of money," says Hartzell. "And soliciting contributions is doubly difficult when half your audience doesn't earn an income."

Nevertheless, SCT has not only survived but thrived. Its burgeoning young audiences have made it the second largest children's theater in the country, and each year it gives away more than $800,000 worth of free or discounted tickets to eligible youth. "We're really a social services agency," quips Hartzell. One of the early Kreielsheimer Foundation grants supported just this kind of needed access. A second-grade teacher in Auburn made an especially poignant request on behalf of her low-income students. After travel expenses, she had only $230 to pay for eighty-nine students, teachers, and parent chaperones. Would it be possible for them to attend at this enormously reduced rate? "It would be a chance for our students to dress up and feel special. It would also allow them to see a side of life that they may not have seen before." Of course the answer was yes.

One month later, another letter arrived at the SCT offices. "Thank you for allowing us to see *Still Life with Iris*," it began. "The children loved it and have not stopped talking about it! I wish you could have seen them all dressed up and trying so hard to be perfect gentlemen and ladies. I thought I was going to cry. . . . Even the parents who did not accompany us are still talking about the trip. I have heard many positive remarks about how special the children felt, how excited they were to see a real play at a real theatre, and how they are suggesting that the whole family should dress up and see a play. . . . It is a day they will remember forever."

Linda Hartzell is passionate about the SCT's place in Northwest cultural life. The Children's Theatre not only provides a live alternative to movies and television, it serves as a feeder for the adult theaters. "The kids that come to our shows grow up and subscribe to the Rep, ACT, Intiman, the Empty Space. . . We give them a thirst for the theater that lasts a lifetime."

The role of the Foundation in helping build the Seattle Children's Theatre, while significant, was not part of the theater's wellspring. After trustee Charles Osborn covered the last small expenses for the "Theatre-In-Sign" project in 1985, he did not respond to SCT's frequent requests for help with its capital project for a new facility on the Seattle Center campus. The campaign for the new theater began in the late 1980s. It was needed because the institution was required to return its old Woodland Park home to the Zoo for the park department's own educational programs. More impressively, the new facility was needed because of the popularity and success of the Seattle Children's Theatre. It needed more seats.

The capital campaign's $8 million goal was advanced first by contributions in 1990 from the City of Seattle (for $2 million), Boeing, the Joshua Green Foundation, and the National Endowment for the Arts, among others. The NEA's important imprimatur came as a challenge grant of $125,000, the same amount it gave that year to children's theaters in Minneapolis, Honolulu, and Louisville, marking them, along with Seattle's, as the best in the land.

Another 1990 gift brought with it a name for the new theater. Somewhat like Abraham Lincoln, Charlotte Martin was raised in a modest log cabin — although in Montana not Illinois — and wound up on Hunts Point (not the White House) living with the largess earned from raising wheat and selling Cadillacs. She gave $1.2 million for the new Charlotte Martin Theatre.

Osborn's reasons for declining to join the parade of this campaign were his common ones at that time. A short list of the larger projects to which he was then committed — most importantly a practice facility for the Pacific Northwest Ballet and his hopes to help build a new concert hall on what he called the K block across Mercer Street from the Opera House

— compelled him to reply, "We are therefore in no position to take on a new commitment at the Seattle Center." The SCT returned to the Foundation in 1993 and greatly impressed Don Johnson, still in his first year of trusteeship, with its artistic quality, management, and perseverance. He made a $500,000 commitment to the Theatre: $400,000 for the capital campaign and the remainder as a match for a $100,000 endowment gift given as a challenge by the Theatre's new namesake, Charlotte Martin.

The last two grants from the Kreielsheimer Foundation reflect both ends of the spectrum of charitable donation. The first, a matching endowment grant of $500,000, honored Linda Hartzell for her artistic and managerial excellence. The second, a $100,000 grant earmarked for season support over three years, supplemented operating expenses with no strings attached. Molly Reed, director of development, recalls, "We had some money left over from previous capital campaigns that we moved into endowment, and Don was one of the first people that we went to . . . It was just so nice of him to recognize the importance of Linda to this organization." Linda adds, "What do you say about somebody who always remembers your name when you know there's fifty million people wanting a piece of them? Don is a hero because he's such a smart, kind person — and he loves the arts . . . He made me feel that what I was doing was important and special and that I should keep doing it."

In total, Kreielsheimer contributions to the Seattle Children's Theatre for its endowment, building, season support, and special needs come to $1,216,305. Finally, Don Johnson's respect for Linda Hartzell, whom he describes as "a miracle worker," also brightened the Foundation's giving to the Seattle Children's Theatre.

A Contemporary Theater

In 1965, Gregory and Jean Falls founded A Contemporary Theatre (ACT) to offer Northwest audiences an alternative to the more established classics that predominated at the Rep. For thirty years, ACT flourished at the base of Queen Anne Hill. The Theatre's many successes had enabled it to pay off the mortgage on its First and Roy digs in 1983, but rehearsal and performance space there was limited. A steadily growing subscriber base filled its 400 seats to capacity. In addition, the older building was crumbling around the edges. It was obvious to ACT management and its board of directors that the Theatre needed to expand. The question was where.

One effort to purchase and develop a location on Second Avenue downtown had failed in the early '90s when the developer went bankrupt. ACT had committed a significant amount of money and effort and the loss was a real blow. The Theatre's formidable board of directors scoured the city for suitable sites. One location that kept appearing on the radar was the gorgeous but dilapidated Eagles Auditorium. Designed by noted Seattle architect and structural engineer Henry Bittman in 1924, the building's terra-cotta ornamentation and Romanesque style made it eligible for landmark status. Don Johnson's office at Bogle & Gates was just across the street and he had always appreciated the Eagles' unique qualities. At the same time, his affection was tempered by knowledge of the many stumbling blocks it presented.

To begin with the building would have to be internally gutted, then seismically retrofitted; another floor had to be added to accommodate housing, while squeezing in two main stages and a couple of smaller performance spaces. Balancing the needs of city planners, housing authorities, landmark commissions, the department of construction and land use, and a theater with a limited budget called for a master juggler. Don recalls "incredible issues involving timing, uncertain costs, various boards issuing assortments of permits . . . I knew they could get totally lost and devoured by delays and bureaucratic red tape." From past experience, Don knew the project would require a huge effort, and that at any time it might turn into "a horror story." But over three or four years, the ACT board and management worked together to solve each problem one at a time and then move on to the next. Don was thrilled to observe their progress. "The perseverance of Susan Trapnell, David Skinner, George Willoughby, Buster Alvord, and some of their other stalwarts impressed me no end." Boeing president Phil Condit, chair of the capital committee, was instrumental in personally bringing the project forward and overcoming seemingly insurmountable obstacles.

With only a couple of hurdles remaining, Condit met Johnson at the Kreielsheimer offices to detail ACT's remarkable progress and to present a formal request for funding. Don was enormously impressed. In his estimation, ACT had reached what he called "a critical mass." Condit proposed that the Foundation start the snowball rolling down the mountain with

Kreielsheimer Place, with the Convention Center in the background

$3 million; in return, the building would be named after the Kreielsheimers. Johnson, who as a boy in Seattle loved nothing more than watching B-17 Flying Fortresses take to the sky, has, he admits, "a soft touch for Boeing." Don looked Condit right in the eye and asked, "Phil, can you get these things done in the next eighteen months?" Yes, said Condit. "In that case," said Don, "we'll be partners. You solve those last problems and we'll give you $3 million. And that's what we did."

In the end, $2 million went toward construction of Kreielsheimer Place and $1 million towards ACT's operating expenses. But Don's influence wasn't limited to the big-ticket items; true to his reputation; he was the consummate man of details. Jim Loder, former financial director of ACT, tells the following tale: "The reason we have a sign on our building is because Don's office was across the street. Every time he looked out his office window, it bothered him that he couldn't tell there was a theater across the street. It looked more like an apartment building. So he marched over here and said, 'What's it going to take to get you people to put a sign on your building?' " Loder protested that they had other, larger issues to worry about. But Don persisted. "He said, 'You're missing the big picture. One of the reasons you're having trouble is because you don't have a sign on your building. So get a sign.' He kept pushing me, literally calling every two weeks. 'Have you made any progress, are you gonna get that sign, show me the proposal.' And then of course, he had the strength of character to put his money where his mouth was and help us fund it."

In the last few months of the Foundation's existence, another million was granted to fund an endowment. And, as it would turn out, the theater needed every penny. Although the new space was widely admired as among the most beautiful theaters in the country, there were bumpy roads ahead. The gorgeous new sign that Kreielsheimer had funded beckoned, but the seats just didn't fill up. And to support two stages, which effectively doubled seating capacity, ACT had to increase its subscriber base. Unfortunately, over the first couple of years, subscriptions dropped. An inexperienced artistic director struggled with her first season. Some subscribers missed the familiar old structure at the base of Queen Anne. Others worried (unnecessarily) about parking downtown. Another, more seasoned artistic director was hired. He mounted expensive new productions, luring top-dollar stars from Broadway and Hollywood. But hoped-for audience increases never materialized. Budget deficits led to debt and finally to insolvency. In early 2003, ACT closed its doors, possibly forever.

With one of its "big three" theaters in mortal danger, the community rallied. Losing ACT meant not just the loss of a single theater but potentially the end of an era. Without all three of the majors, many theater artists realized that Seattle might no longer be able to support them. There were heroes. Susan Trapnell, who had moved on to other jobs, came back to Seattle to head up the last-ditch fund-raising campaign. Kurt Beattie assumed the mantle of artistic director and joined the fray. And over a period of weeks, despite a brutal economy, donations large and small poured in in time to meet an April 15 deadline. A month later, ACT announced a new, though truncated, season.

Since then, ACT has checked itself out of intensive care and anticipates a full recovery. Susan Trapnell returned to her position as managing director, and, with Kurt Beattie at the artistic helm along with the ministrations of a cautious but responsive board of directors, is guiding the theater back to solvency and full subscriptions. At this writing, ACT is moving successfully through its second season after reopening, and Susan Trapnell reports that the theatre hopes to balance its books for the first time in several years.

Footlight Footnotes

In Seattle and around the world theatres struggle to survive through good times and bad. When I asked about the ultimate contribution of the Kreielsheimer Foundation, several responses revealed a mix of gratitude and mourning.

"I watched Don really grow into this role . . . if you sit back and take a snapshot of the Foundation and say, in the end what has it accomplished, it has to be a pretty impressive story." — Jim Tune

"Don was so helpful. He would sit down and say, 'What do you need?' . . . He wasn't coming in as an outsider but as a true collaborator. Now there's nobody out there." — Pam Schell

"There's nothing around that remotely replaces Kreielsheimer's impact over the last fifteen years. Charlie and Don, each in their own way, assured that the Kreielsheimer influence should be writ large." — Melissa Hines

4 | Dance

Genevieve McCoy

Pacific Northwest Ballet

"It was truly a windfall for us," wrote Pacific Northwest Ballet's Karla Steel to Charles Osborn in 1981, thanking him for the $10,000 Foundation contribution for set construction costs in their production of *Swan Lake*. The ballet company was a little over eight years old and, like so many arts organizations in the early 1980s in Seattle, struggling to establish itself and to grow. Founded under the aegis of the Seattle Opera in 1973, the Pacific Northwest Ballet Association in its first seasons performed solely in operas and watched its first two artistic directors leave after only one year. It was not until 1975 that the organization mounted eight performances of its own of the full-length *Nutcracker* ballet and started operating its school. That year the company, based in the Good Shepherd Center in Wallingford, originally a shelter home for young girls, consisted of eighteen dancers and the school of 150 students. The annual budget was a mere $420,000.

The turning point for the fledging ballet company came with the arrival of Kent Stowell and Francia Russell. Each had trained in the style of George Balanchine, one of the foremost ballet choreographers of the twentieth century. Stowell and Russell began as artistic directors during the 1977–78 season and immediately set about transforming the company into what would become within the next ten years the nationally recognized Pacific Northwest Ballet, or PNB. Finding and training the best dancers, Stowell and Russell knew, would be only one aspect of the immense challenges facing them. In order to build Seattle's first professional ballet company, they recognized that gaining the recognition and support of the local arts community for a modernist form of plotless ballet could be a formidable undertaking.

By 1986 PNB's forty-two-dancer troop and 400 students were pushing the limits of the Good Shepherd Center studios. Fortunately, two years

45

earlier, the Ballet had acquired in Arthur Jacobus a president with the expertise and skills to successfully lead a $5 million capital campaign to build a new facility. When Jacobus and Lynn Shrader, PNB's development manager, first met with Charles Osborn in August 1985, the Kreielsheimer trustee was skeptical that the Seattle-area community would ever support such a sizable campaign goal. Even though he agreed that the Ballet needed new quarters, he was surely not convinced that the Foundation should become PNB's principal campaign donor.

In August 1988 Osborn met again with several PNB representatives, who were feeling pressed to quickly raise $2 million in order to exercise their option on the Seattle Center's Exhibition Hall for the Ballet's new home by the city's late-September deadline. After one of the PNB trustees proposed a $5 million Foundation gift for the undertaking, the trustee was nearly struck speechless. This was quickly reduced to "What about $3 million," then $1.25 million. Osborn was still aghast at the size of the requests, but he was more than willing to give the Foundation's "fair share" toward the project. In fact, as he noted for the file, the Foundation's gift of $300,000 would amount to 4.5 percent of the $7.5 million cost of the building renovation. All told, the Foundation's gift was second only in size to that of the Boeing Company among all the contributors. Later, pleased that the construction on the Exhibition Hall was proceeding on time and on budget, and knowing that the failure of the Seattle Center Levy in May 1991 would cost the Ballet a significant source of funding, the trustee pledged another $200,000 toward the hall renovation on a two-to-one matching basis.

Charles Osborn had proposed the matching grant to Arthur Jacobus as a way to encourage more donors to make their gifts more speedily. The plan worked, for the ballet company both met the Foundation challenge grant and completed Phase II of the construction on budget and on time by the end of 1991. As Jacobus put it in a letter thanking Osborn in December 1991: "The Kreielsheimer Foundation's Challenge grant was particularly effective in motivating our volunteers [and donors] by creating a sense of urgency. As a result, we saw second gifts, quicker giving decisions, and accelerated payment schedules." Because the half-million-dollar Foundation money was instrumental in raising other funds for construction, by the end of the campaign in July 1992 the Ballet had secured over

$11 million for its new home, the Phelps Center, which would increase the company's studio, facility, and administrative space by nearly 200 percent. For their vital support, PNB named one of the studios after Leo and Greye Kreielsheimer and installed a memorial plaque to honor Charles F. Osborn for his "critical development role" in establishing the new facility.

A few months after the passing of the first trustee in the late summer of 1992, Don Johnson accompanied Harriet Osborn, Charlie's widow, to the opening of the Phelps Center in the spring of 1993. It was there, during PNB Artistic Director Francia Russell's remarks to the celebrants, that Johnson learned the story of how Osborn had initiated the gift. Johnson recounts, "That night I was impressed with Francia Russell's grace and articulation. And so, I learned, was Charlie. It was in the course of thanking three or four major supporters like the Legislature and Sheffield Phelps and his family that Francia came to Charlie. She recalled that Osborn had phoned and said, 'Let me help out.' When she asked 'How much can you give?' he replied, 'That is not the question. The question is how much do you need?' What they got was $500,000, and a half a million was a good-sized grant then." Charles Osborn's correction of Francia Russell's question is an instance of the Foundation's actively inquiring interest in helping out with rescues.

To Don Johnson the Foundation's support of the PNB is an example of how it often approached the major fine arts groups, ballet included. "It has always been an objective to focus on trying to shore up groups that are in difficulties of a kind that is curable and not terminal. Kreielsheimer had the ability to step in and maybe make something happen that wouldn't have happened because other resources were just not there." Johnson continued to monitor the Ballet's progress and to send it crucial dollars. The 1993 $25,000 grant for Stowell's *Fauré Requiem*, a tribute to Balanchine on the tenth anniversary of his death, enabled the company to balance its 1992–93 budget. The 1994–96 Foundation grants, totaling a quarter million dollars, played a crucial role in supporting the Ballet's repertory and school during the mid-1990s.

By 1995 PNB was receiving the national and international attention it so well deserved. That year it was the fifth largest ballet company in the country, in terms of number of dancers and length of season, and it had the highest per-capita attendance of any ballet company in the nation. In the late 1990s encomiums for its reinterpretation of Balanchine's rendition of Shakespeare's *A Midsummer Night's Dream* (the first reconceptualization of the ballet ever attempted) appeared wherever it was staged—from Seattle (where it premiered in May 1997), to New York, Edinburgh, and London, bolstering the company's reputation greatly. However, the $1.2 million production costs, funded in part by a $100,000 Kreielsheimer grant, along with tour expenses, had made the ballet one of PNB's most expensive productions ever.

Well aware of the difficulties of dance organizations' ability to meet programmatic and artistic goals while raising money to pay for them, Don Johnson in 1996 began encouraging the PNB to set up a permanent endowment that would secure the Ballet a regular annual income, as well as underscore its growing institutional status and financial credibility for the philanthropic community. With an endowment, he argued, the Ballet would be assured of regular scholarship funds to finance its community outreach programs and nurture promising dancers like its principal, Patricia Barker; it would be better able to build a superior repertory by creating and commissioning new works; and an endowment would create a secure cultural legacy for both the audiences and artists of tomorrow.

Ballerina Barker is another example of an edifying influence on Johnson the art lover and gift-giver. Most likely one of the reasons that the Foundation partnered with local dance is the admiration Don Johnson felt for Barker's dancing. In his "humble opinion"—and the trustee emphasizes the "humble"—"Patty Barker is the ultimate ballet dancer." It was of course fine for the PNB to have such an influential fan. It also explains the Foundation's preference for funding performances by a local group rather than a "presentation" of a touring ballet like the Bolshoi Ballet through a Seattle "presenter" like the Paramount or the 5th Avenue Theatre or even the University of Washington's Meany Hall for the Performing Arts, all of which have at times staged imported dance programs. Johnson explains, "Now it is great to bring in the world's best performers, but Leo Kreielsheimer's preference was to help build the Washington State–based institutions."

The $1 million 1997 Kreielsheimer Endowment for the Arts and Education Program grant, a hundred times larger than its initial Foundation grant, was a true windfall for PNB. It was to be used specifically "to fund new work or otherwise artistically challenging dance programs that

Patricia Barker, prima ballerina of the Pacific Northwest Ballet

would be difficult or impossible for PNB to accomplish within its regular operating budget." The stiff, two-to-one matching terms were, like those of Osborn's earlier grant, intended to spur greater fund-raising efforts and quicker contributions. By May of 2000, the Ballet reported it had achieved its $10 million endowment campaign goal.

Conditions were not wholly buoyant for the Ballet, however. Small annual budget deficits, in part due to government cuts in arts support, periodic reduced box-office sales, the frequent turnover of fiscal managers and board trustees, and the difficulty of maintaining a solid donor base continued to challenge the Ballet in the late 1990s. In response to these problems, the PNB board of trustees in 2000 reorganized itself to focus more solidly on fund-raising, and hired a new executive director, D. David Brown, formerly with the Boston Ballet. When Brown wrote Don Johnson requesting more endowment support, Johnson hesitated for a moment because of the Ballet's recent precarious financial condition. But only for a moment. For after considering his long association with PNB and directors Russell and Stowell, the trustee decided to trust his instincts and "just bet the million" on them once more. As he closed out the Foundation funds in 2000, he made another $1,000,000 endowment pledge to PNB, this time with no strings attached. Ultimately, the Kreielsheimer Foundation's total support for the ballet amounted to in excess of $3.5 million.

On the Boards

By the early 1990s On the Boards (OTB) was internationally recognized as Seattle's most avant-garde sponsor of contemporary performance art, but it was badly in need of a new home, having long outgrown its rented quarters in Washington Hall on First Hill.* Johnson became familiar with OTB and their needs while working with ACT in its move to its new Kreielsheimer Place home in the renovated Eagles Auditorium. For its own fund-raising, ACT figured the value of its original lower Queen Anne quarters into the sum it needed to raise. The price ACT set was $1,650,000; and with OTB facing a competing commercial offer for the property, it needed the kind of help that only a few years earlier would have seemed downright bold for even the largest established performing groups. However, with yet another chance to save another stage while helping On the Boards, the Foundation joined a long list of philanthropic activists to answer the call.

With faith in the financial expertise of Managing Director Sara Pasti and the OTB board, in October 1996 Johnson pledged an initial $150,000 one-to-one challenge, hoping that OTB could buy the building from the theater company before it went on the market. After a strenuous whirlwind campaign, OTB successfully matched the grant in December, a mere two months later. OTB's $4 million capital campaign was so productive that Johnson made a second challenge award of $350,000. When he met with Pasti at the theater renovation site in August 1998, she told him that "without the Kreielsheimer gift, particularly the initial $150,000 gift that enabled us to secure the agreement of ACT Theater to sell us the property, the whole project would not have been possible." The work of creating the necessary critical mass to keep the theater a venue for the arts was made considerably easier by the many fond memories for the building associated with the ACT group's more than thirty years there.

Besides the Kreielsheimer Foundation, the list of individuals, corporations, foundations, and governmental agencies that came together to complete On the Boards' $4.2 million campaign in record time is a who's who of local philanthropy. Among the committed were Boeing, Microsoft, the Allen Foundation for the Arts, the Bagley Wright Fund, the National Endowment for the Arts, the Kresge Foundation, Kayla Skinner, the King

* On the Boards is also considered in chapter 14 of this book.

County Cultural Facilities Fund/Hotel-Motel Tax Revenues, the state's Building for the Arts Program, Paul Brainerd and Kenneth and Marlene Alhadeff and, of course, the Behnke family. Johnson recalls, "When the Behnkes (John and Shari and John's parents, Robert and Sally) came forward and matched the Foundation's gift I was asked, 'Is it okay if we call it the Behnke Center for the Performing Arts?' I answered, 'Of course.' The truth is, the Foundation has never been name-happy. Our 'name story' is this. In those places where the Kreielsheimer name does appear it was never embraced by the Foundation at the expense of another gift. Frankly, I've known the Behnke and Skinner families for many years, and if anyone deserves recognition it is they, considering all that they have done for Seattle arts and other community programs over the years."

In October 1998 On the Boards launched its twentieth season in the new facility. ACT's semicircular seating was replaced with steep risers because, as On the Boards' artistic director, Mark Murphy, explained to Misha Berson, *Seattle Times* theater critic, "In dance, which is about sixty percent of what we do, you have to see the whole body from head to toe." Before performances and at intermissions, patrons gather in the Kreielsheimer Main Lobby.

Other Dance and Performance Art Projects

Beyond its effective attentions to the Pacific Northwest Ballet and On the Boards, the Kreielsheimer Foundation also touched in smaller ways on the productions of several other performing arts organizations for whom dance was either the first interest or nearly so. With work somewhat like that of OTB, the UMO Ensemble, centered on Vashon Island, has a tradition of encouraging and in its case creating experimental productions. In 1999 the UMO received $10,000 from the Foundation for its *Millennium Circus* and its "breathtaking aerial virtuosity." Of the $36,000 total received from the Foundation, the greater and last part of it, $25,000, was given in 2000 as a "new works grant." It was evidence of the Foundation's admiration for the daring of the UMO's original creations.

With the financial help received from the Foundation in 1993, Spectrum Dance Theater, Seattle's only professional jazz dance company, was for the first time able to mount two ambitious concert series at Meany

Hall, receiving its first dance review in *Dance Magazine.* That same year Co-Motion, the Northwest's oldest repertory modern dance company, founded in 1978, was awarded a small Foundation grant, in order to renovate its new studio and informal performance space in Pioneer Square. With her dance company Homenaje, Sara de Luis performed *Sara and Her Lovers* at the Leo K. Theatre in 1999. It was the farewell performance for the popular local classical Spanish dancer, and another example of the Foundation's capacity to step forward and support a project that might otherwise have had a difficult time finding funding.

The Alaska Dance Theatre was one of the several arts-related organizations in Alaska supported by the Foundation. Founded in 1983 by five women with a dream to build a dance school and performing organization, Alaska Dance Theatre soon outgrew its original Quonset hut home on the Alaska Pacific University campus and even its second shared facility in Anchorage. In 1993 the organization purchased The Dance Center on Gambell Street and began the difficult task of building not only the school and the ballet company, but also financing the mortgage on the center. ADT had little savings and was heavily dependent on community funds to make the down payment on the building. By 1997, with a $279,000 mortgage balloon payment looming, the newly hired executive director, Michele Miller, was seeking to pay off the mortgage and find more favorable refinancing to make ADT's home secure. Among others, she turned to Don Johnson and the Kreielsheimer Foundation for help, explaining that ADT was the largest dance organization in Alaska, serving a student body of over 500 and supporting thirty dancers in forty-five annual public performances. Even though the organization had secured a board of trustees, public cuts to arts funding, and the difficulty cultivating a philanthropic arts community for the support of dance in Alaska, made fund-raising a particular challenge. Don Johnson recognized these difficulties and in May 1998 offered ADT a $37,500 Foundation challenge grant on a one-to-three matching basis to aid in fund-raising efforts to pay off the mortgage on The Dance Center building. Although they required a deadline extension, ADT met the challenge and raised the additional $112,500 by the middle of 2000.

Part II

Notable Capital Projects

Most larger capital projects in the arts require prolonged nurturing within a community's circle of philanthropists. Success follows a clasping of two hands, the private and the public. The Seattle Symphony's new performance hall got its early spark from Kreielsheimer, and, following a second extraordinary ignition from the Benaroya family and a third from Boeing, the public's part became a felt necessity and the city soon joined in. This charmed scenario holds true for the Opera House as well. After the early commitment from the Foundation was followed by both the McCaw and Brotman commitments, the public side responded at every level: state, county, and city—especially the city, beginning with the passing of the 1999 Seattle Center levy that put aside $29 million for the project. Although the expected contributions were subsequently retarded by the general trauma of September 11 (the terrorist attack on New York and the Pentagon) and the regional recession accompanying the dot.com sag, they did not stop.

Especially in Seattle, these big arts projects seem touched by an irresistible charm or community chemistry that will have its way. The proof of this political alchemy occurred late in 2002. Even in a time of significant recession, the critical mass to make something happen had reached a major juncture and would not be denied. After both private and public funds lagged—only $4 million of the combined $17 million promised by King County and the state had been delivered—the Seattle City Council made a $27 million bridge loan to guarantee that the Opera House would be finished on time. As a precedent this rescue was controversial, but new Mayor Greg Nickels promised that if the loan and its interest could not ultimately be paid for by donations that they would then be met by adding fees to ticket prices.

Chapter 5 tracks the extended story of what became familiar as the "K block." Twice the Foundation followed its hopes for the joined parcels it purchased across Mercer Street from the Seattle Center downtown as first the Seattle Art Museum and then also the Seattle Symphony's new performance hall became important parts of the revitalization of the Central Business District. Yet ultimately the twists and turns in this story of Seattle's largest capital projects in the arts brought the Kreielsheimer

Foundation back to the Seattle Center and new visions for its K block as well as to the elegant splendor of its namesake promenade. Chapter 6 returns for another look into two large capital projects already described in chapter 2, and concludes with a listing of other notable capital projects that involved the Foundation. Directions are also included to guide the reader to locations in the book where more detailed treatments of the significance of these projects are found.

5 | On and Off Mercer Street

When he began purchasing the parcels of the K block Charles Osborn, ordinarily the modest giver and prudent trustee, performed like a visionary but within the context of a local and venerable tradition. Osborn became an impassioned advocate for extending the already considerable legacy of Seattle Center as a reserve for arts and culture—a center that was some distance from the city's other center, its Central Business District.

After four years of his early incremental purchases, Osborn deeded the $2.15 million Mercer Street parcel to the city, but with the stipulation that something be built there for "cultural and educational purposes within four years." On February 20, 1986, *Seattle Times* music critic Melinda Bargreen wondered, "The City's got it. Now what are they going to do with it?" Osborn's first hope for the nearly 43,000 square feet he had assembled was that the Seattle Art Museum would build its new home on this charmed site. This was part of the trustee's vision of Seattle Center as the city's secure destination for its major players: its symphony, opera, ballet, and a new art museum. When the Seattle Art Museum soon chose its downtown corner instead Osborn was shaken. Perhaps feeling both emboldened and entitled by recent contributions of nearly $1 million to SAM, he wrote an eight-page choleric epistle to all the members of the City Council that became—inevitably—also an open letter to the community. Osborn included a long list of reasons why he thought the downtown site a bad one, but his strongest point was also his oldest one: that SAM could have saved itself all the costs connected with the new downtown site if they had just taken the Kreielsheimer gift beside Seattle Center.

Within a month of Osborn's bold letter, Bargreen wrote an exposition of the Foundation's work with a tone that developed its own crescendo. It began "quietly at first, then with increasing prominence, the money has begun to surface in the arts community . . . Where is the money coming from? Who controls it, and how is it being used?" The answer was Osborn. In the accompanying portrait, his arms folded, Charles Osborn looks resolutely into the camera. While the photograph has a caption — "Osborn is described as outspoken" — the story's big punning headline, "The Buck Stops Here," takes the lead in defining this portrait of a confident trustee with attitude. In the article Osborn is described by Irwin Treiger, at the time another Bogle & Gates attorney, as "a man of absolute, impeccable integrity and honesty . . . He calls things as he sees them."*

Osborn's revelations to Bargreen included a sympathetic description of Leo Kreielsheimer. "I knew what he wanted. . . . He was a very interesting and very outgoing individual who had excellent relationships with all his employees. He was generous and responsive to the needs of the Kodiak community (the site of the Kreielsheimer canneries), and had the affection of all the people there, from the guy who opens the doors on the plane to the hospital personnel. He was well read, with a photographic memory. A few years before his death, he went to Westminster Abbey for the first time, but he already knew so much about it that when someone asked him for directions, a crowd gathered around him, thinking he was an official guide." Osborn goes on to describe Greye Kreielsheimer as "deeply interested in the arts, and very knowledgeable. She shared that interest with her husband." Most revealingly, Leo Kreielsheimer's will includes the founder's description of their intentions. "The Trustees should bear in mind the interests that my wife and I have in the support and further development of the fine arts, museums, libraries, drama and the like . . . as it is our joint desire that the Foundation be primarily concerned with the maintenance and development of cultural and educational institutions in the Northwest, and particularly in Western Washington."†

Charles Osborn's acerbic letter to the City Council was one example of how far the trustee would go to "bear in mind" Leo and Greye's interests, and probably his own as well. His bold diligence in investigating the alternative site chosen by the Museum impressed the *Times* critic. "Osborn doesn't oppose the downtown site out of sheer orneriness or a desire to be different. In what appears to be his characteristic way, he has formed an impassioned opinion after extensive financial analysis of the Museum's assets, equities, pledges, and debt-servicing projections — and after walking

---

* For more on Charles Osborn, see chapter 18.

† The creation, structure, and philosophy of the Foundation are discussed in chapter 15.

and driving around the downtown site repeatedly, both at day and at night. This is not the kind of behavior you expect of your average senior-citizen attorney." On one such exploration, Osborn explained that he watched "two hoods opening both doors of the car in front of me, with a male driver alone in the car." Osborn honked his horn several times and started out of his own vehicle, and "the hoods ran off." Clearly Charlie Osborn was afraid for the welfare of those visiting the Museum and on one occasion referred directly to how his wife, Harriet, shared his aversion to the location on a First Avenue that was then still characterized as "Flesh Avenue." The idea that attending a show at the new SAM might require one to park near the Lusty Lady Theater was not comforting. However, the fact was that long before SAM began construction on this site of the old Arcade Building, First Avenue and the Pike Place Public Market Neighborhood were well into gentrification. It was a cleanup that the new museum would add to mightily. With SAM in the neighborhood the dominos of reclassification began to fall — or rather rise — across First Avenue with the Harbor Steps development and across Second Avenue with Benaroya Hall. Bonnie Pitman-Gelles, the Museum's acting director in 1986, defended the Museum trustees' expensive choice over Osborn's gift by talking directly to this point of urban renewal. "We are committed to the revitalization of downtown." Pitman-Gelles described Osborn's prescription as "just a different agenda."

When neither the City Council nor Museum administrators remained faithful to the block he was preparing for them, Osborn withdrew the $5 million ten-year plan offered to the Museum for its expansion program (although SAM would continue to receive other grants from the Foundation) and reluctantly but swiftly turned his attention to the next best chance for the K block. The Museum of History and Industry was the substitute first suggested by the Seattle Center. Osborn declined. Rather, as his successor Don Johnson describes it, "Charlie proposed the use of the K block for the symphony concert hall and he was a leader in providing funding for preliminary designs." The Opera House was overbooked. As Symphony Director Gerard Schwarz characterized it, the Seattle performing arts family had begat too many children for its home. A concert-hall advisory committee headed by Dr. Kermit O. Hanson was organized late in 1987 to visit other halls around the country and to report back to Osborn.

The Foundation published the findings in a spiral-bound chapbook with a vivid red cover — which became known as "The Red Book." A cream-and-gray model of the Symphony Hall was unveiled on May 25, 1989.[+]

At that time, the orchestra's heaviest hitters, philanthropist and auto-parts magnate Sam Stroum and Richard P. Cooley, SeaFirst chief executive officer, were preoccupied with reversing the orchestra's practice of accumulating annual debts in the low millions. Stroum was an "eyeball to eyeball" fundraiser and he had the Kreielsheimer Foundation in his gaze more for operating expenses than for a new home. In the spring of 1988 Charles Osborn confided to Melissa Bargreen, "Mr. Stroum has already visited me and twisted my arm a little. And when Sam Stroum visits you, you listen seriously to what he has to say." Osborn prudently extended for another two years the time the city was allowed to assemble the friends and forces required to build a new symphony hall. That these powers required another eight years suggests that Osborn's alternative vision for his K block was premature. The delay was also evidence of Seattle's reputation as the "Capital of Process." Extensions were repeatedly asked for by the city and given by the Foundation — the last of these by Johnson, for Charles Osborn did not live long enough to track the development of his Seattle Symphony proposal for the dearly bought property facing Mercer Street.

Don Johnson's affection for the concert hall site was downright personal. He grew up in Magnolia, not far from the Center. "I went to Queen Anne High School. You could almost throw a rock from there down onto that land. I went to teenage dances in the old Civic Auditorium. I watched Adlai Stevenson make a speech there in 1956. About Charlie's block I said, 'I know that. That is like home to me down there.' Within two days after Charlie's passing I privately knew that there was no way that I was going to terminate. But to say that outright would have been, you might say, a 'disincentive' to the city to keep moving along." Johnson waited ten weeks to reveal his K-block decision on the occasion of Mayor Norm Rice's address to the Bogle & Gates firm at a November lunch at the Rainier Club. "I went up to him afterwards and I said, 'Well, Mr. Mayor I have here a letter

+ Designed by Loschky Marquardt & Nesholm, it was later modified to fit the chosen downtown site as Benaroya Hall. For more on the Red Book and related K-block subjects, see chapters 1 and 22.

that will please you. We are going to extend the time.' I added something like, 'I believe in the concert hall every bit as much as Charles Osborn did.' When I handed it to him he gave me a bear hug like Norm Rice can do." Johnson, however, gave the embraceable Rice only one year to respond, not the two that Charles Osborn regularly offered the city if they made some show of progress towards developing the K-block property.

The shortened K-block extension was granted in part because of the economic echoes still felt from the clanging failure of the $94.3 million Seattle Center levy. Even though the levy failed, some renovation at Seattle Center was still allowed. What had happened was that proponents of the levy failed to convince voters in the hinterlands of King County to vote for support of additions like a new symphony hall. The Orchestra's 1991–92 season opened on September 13 — a Friday — with Mahler's Third Symphony. The following June orchestra management warned that the season's shortfall could pass a half million. By year's end, the baroque complexity of building a prosperous orchestra required what its administrators termed "a plan for a plan." Happily, before the 1992–93 symphony season concluded, its new "metaplan" found its own superman.

In the late spring of 1993 the mellifluous Symphony announced a $15.8 million gift for the construction of a new performance hall. It seems that the Foundation's veteran tracker, *Seattle Times* critic Bargreen, indirectly influenced Jack Benaroya in his decision to join the campaign through the story she wrote on Johnson's assumption of the Kreielsheimer trusteeship. While on a Palm Desert vacation, Benaroya read of Johnson's impassioned commitment to sticking with the Symphony's campaign to build a new hall on the K block. While Benaroya was no stranger to the Symphony — he was a friend of Maestro Schwarz — nevertheless the story of the Kreielsheimer Foundation and its new trustee's dedication moved the senior Benaroya to remark to himself, "Well I think that project needs a little help." Normally we only encounter such understated and yet heroic thoughts framed in cartoon bubbles floating above the muscular figures of conscientious superheroes. For about a week before the announcement a rumor of a large grant from an anonymous donor made the rounds of the arts community. Over lunch at the Rainier Club it was suddenly revealed to Don Johnson how a rumor can unfurl into fact.

Jack Benaroya's lawyer Irwin Treiger (an art activist in his own right) was Don Johnson's partner at Bogle & Gates. As Johnson recalls it, "Irwin called me on the interoffice phone on a Friday morning and said, 'Don, would you like to have lunch with *the anonymous donor?*' Irwin knew that I was helping lead the charge for the symphony hall. I said 'Yes, of course,' and on Monday we met at the Rainer Club. There was Jack Benaroya. Jack asked 'Would you mind if the concert hall was named for the Benaroya Family?' I answered, 'Jack for $15.8 million dollars I wouldn't mind that one bit.' So that is how it happened." According to Johnson the commitment of the Benaroya family "really kicked things up to a fever pitch."

With its great new friend, the Symphony's sanguine time was made healthier still in early December 1993, when the Musical America International/Directory of the Performing Arts named Seattle Symphony's musical director, Gerald Schwarz, Conductor of the Year. Later that month the orchestra awarded LMN Architects the contract to design a new Benaroya Hall. The K block was still the site imagined, and the expectation that soon the Symphony's new home would extend the Seattle Center campus felt for some like a renaissance of the "Seattle Spirit" felt during Century 21. As a member of the capital committee for the new hall of which Bagley Wright was the chair, Johnson notes, "I spent at least a third of my time through early 1994 on the symphony project." Soon, however, he would have some free time.

A downtown site for a new symphony hall became more than the preference of some when an advisory group recommended it early in July. A public debate on this controversial selection continued through the summer. In late September a letter appeared in the *Seattle Times* with a headline "Reasons Given For Rejecting Gift Horse Inadequate So Far." The gift horse, of course, was the K block. Remembering Charles Osborn's disappointment over the similar move made earlier by the museum, Don Johnson was naturally not happy with the orchestra's decision, although he understood both its advantages and its costs. "The central business district was then in a slump. Frederick & Nelson had closed, I. Magnin moved out, the hotels were nervous, restaurant attendance was down, and Nordstrom was complaining. The membership of the Downtown Seattle Association was troubled. The Symphony's move downtown was done in part for urban renewal. And it worked. It turned out pretty well."

The auditorium at Benaroya Hall

Ironically, the same liabilities of being downtown that Charles Osborn had earlier explored and listed in hopes that the new art museum would be built uptown on the K block were also what lured the Symphony away from Seattle Center. The increasing physical decrepitude and public abandonment of a downtown that at night cab drivers called a "ghost town" made the difference. Like SAM before it, the Seattle Symphony enlisted in the renewal of the area. The final cost of building downtown across Second Avenue from SAM was approximately twice the $67 million projected for the new symphony hall, had it been built beside Seattle Center. Still, the money was raised and the Central Business District renewed.

On September 26, 2000, six days after the Foundation concluded its regular work, the Seattle Symphony announced not only that Benaroya Hall had been paid for but also that the orchestra's endowment fund had also been considerably enlarged. The total capital campaign for both reached $159 million. In this, as happened with the Seattle Art Museum, the Foundation did not end up playing the major part that had been imagined for it for so long by so many. The fund-raising continued, of course, after the Benaroya gift. Boeing soon added $3 million to the building fund.

However, most of the new hall's downtown neighbors did not come forward to help complete it although it was they who would most benefit from the presence of this grand institution. When the soliciting had but three months left to run to meet the minimum fund-raising goal set by the city to permit construction to commence in 1996, the capital campaign was still more than $13 million short of the required harvest. If the symphony team failed to raise it, as Johnson imagined, "the site might have been left with a hole in the ground for another ten years. It was then," he recalls, "that I was expecting a call."

For three hours Don Johnson and Bruce H. "Gus" Cleveland, who handled the bank trustee's Foundation account and so was the principal manager of its investments, met with a Symphony group that included Jack Benaroya and Board President Jean Gardner. "They asked for $10 million but I offered $5 million, citing other major needs in the arts community." Johnson observed that Gardner was visibly shaken not to have come away with the full $10 million. By then the trustee was both experienced and philosophical. Enthused grantees that have received funds are often so enlivened with the value of their projects that they are naturally inclined to want and sometimes expect more. Johnson always kept in mind that the Foundation's resources were limited, and the more costly the project the greater the circumspection. Moreover the $5 million offered to the concert hall was at the time the second largest gift drawn from a local source. "Never before," the trustee reflected, "had the Foundation received no perceptible thanks for a $5 million gift offer." With candor, Johnson explains, "I did not abandon the Symphony; I never would. Bagley Wright was the chairman of the big gifts capital committee, and it was a great success. It wasn't that it didn't struggle. They all struggle. But it also made it."

Included in the package of last gifts to the Seattle Symphony — made on the eve of the Foundation's closing — was $2 million for support of the Soundbridge Learning Center. It is the only part of Benaroya Hall with which the Kreielsheimer name is directly connected. A small plaque indicates that it was made possible by donations from both the Foundation and from Craig and Joan Watjen. The Watjen gift had its source in Microsoft, the region's greatest story of prosperity and also one of its deepest philanthropic pockets. More than one wag has described Soundbridge as our "Experience Classical Music Project." Johnson explains, "They got a consortium of geniuses around town including Bob Herbold, executive vice-president of Microsoft, to put together the software. Go in there sometime. I was amazed. I listened to parts of four versions of Beethoven's Fifth played by four world-class orchestras, including the Seattle Symphony. There was a considerable difference, especially in meter. One version runs fifty-eight minutes and another over an hour. It shows how different conductors interpret the same passage."

From its first grant of $10,000 in 1982 to help its administrators make the conversion to computers to its last grant in 2000, the Foundation gave in all $10,743,867 to the Seattle Symphony Orchestra. Of that total, the $4,743,300 that appears on the Foundation's accounting of its Seattle Symphony grants has a poignant quality. Described as an "opportunity value," the nearly $5 million represents the "loss of income from security market investments in regard to the holding of the K block as the site for the new concert hall from 4/10/86 to 12/31/95." It is the last chapter in what had been intended to be the principal incentive in energizing and keeping alive the community efforts during those years to build a new concert hall for the orchestra. Grants given from 1996 to 2000 focused on other needs of the orchestra.

In 1997 the Kreielsheimer Foundation, along with the private philanthropists Dr. Ellsworth (Buster) and Nancy Alvord and Seattle composer Alan Hovhaness were given that year's Arts Award by the Symphony at its Symphoneve Gala.

When funding for Benaroya Hall reached what Don Johnson likes to call critical mass, he returned with a plan for Mercer Street. "We needed a new opera house on the level of the new concert hall. I went to Mayor Paul Schell with the news that I could budget $15 million and gave him a draft letter. The strategy was that we must get the expiring Seattle Center levy renewed in 1999, otherwise there would likely be no public funding for making changes to the Opera House. Those in charge of the project, the mayor and Virginia Anderson and her staff, felt that if we announced it beforehand it might tempt some voters to say, 'Oh they can do it and we don't have to.' It was a wise strategy, for the levy passed and $29 million worth of public funding was joined to the Kreielsheimer gift." With these joined public and private contributions, the last great capital project of the local "golden age" of arts approached critical mass. Half a year later, the by-reputation somewhat remote McCaw brothers, Bruce, Craig, John, and Keith — a Northwest quartet of exceedingly deep pockets, added another $20 million. The new performance center seemed assured, or nearly so.

In the interim between the two announcements there was — or might have been — a moment of crisis over what to call it. Seattle Center Director Virginia Anderson, who was by Johnson's description "the ex-officio member of everything that is going on," had told him that the new facility ought to be named for the Kreielsheimer family. Anderson told the trustee, "You've got the name unless you are willing to let it go." It was, of course, a good wager that the team playing Johnson would be "willing to let it go" if the community called. And after the McCaw offer was made contingent on naming rights Anderson came to call. She recalls, "That was one of the hardest things I have ever had to do. Don and I went through the Benaroya Hall move together, which was very painful for both of us. Out of the blue from the McCaw family comes their gift specifically for their mother. I told them that I had been negotiating with Don, and that I could not go back on that. They were very respectful. Then I went to Don. There was no other way to say it than to say it straight. 'This is what has happened. You have been with me this whole time. I will honor your commitment and the Opera and Ballet will do the same. Unless you encourage us to accept the McCaw offer.' I also assured Don that if he declined it would not come out and embarrass him. It was very hard initially for both of us, and we talked a lot about that earlier experience with the Symphony."

Following close on the heels of the Benaroya experience this new name exchange was for Don Johnson "déjà vu all over again." The trustee revealed his decision while catching a car ride with William P. "Bill" Gerberding, the retired University of Washington president, and at the time a member of the Opera Board helping with the fund-raising for the new hall. Johnson told Gerberding, "I cannot deny the community $20 million for this project over a naming opportunity. I don't think that Leo Kreielsheimer would have wanted that. It would not be the right thing to do. The Foundation was not created to build their name. They have gotten plenty of posthumous public relations and probably more than they would have liked. I propose that you go ahead with the arrangement with the McCaws." That settled it: the name would be the Marion Oliver McCaw Hall.

It helped that Johnson thought the new Opera House's namesake a "great lady" and likened her to both Katherine Graham of the *Washington Post* and Dorothy Bullitt of King Broadcasting, two women who, like Marion Oliver McCaw, were thrown into the breach of managing media when their husbands died young. In McCaw's case it had meant taking control of a radio station in Chehalis while raising her four teenage sons. Ultimately, her boys created McCaw Cellular. Johnson figures, "That would not have happened without Marion's mentoring." Two years following his ride with Gerberding Johnson added "And boy, we needed the $20 million because we still have $17 million to go."

The possibility that the performance hall auditorium might be named for the Foundation was abandoned when Jeffrey and Susan Brotman, also friends of Don Johnson, gave $5 million to the fund and received the honor of naming the streamlined 2,900 seat auditorium for Susan. And with the new hall's forecourt a special variety of poetic justice was fulfilled. The Kreielsheimer Promenade creates a grand new entry off of Mercer Street to the Center grounds. Virginia Anderson was again appreciative of Don Johnson's foresight. "Very few donors would have understood conceptually how that space could be wonderful not simply because it was the forecourt for the Opera House but because it was the entrance to the campus. But Don understood it—in part because he had made so many investments in so many parts of the campus."

6 | "Critical Mass": Two Examples

Although not on as large a scale as Seattle's recent outsize campaigns, the efforts and talents required to build a new Bellevue Art Museum (BAM) shared some similarities. The Foundation played an important part and Don Johnson, who did the nurturing, considers the ultimate mix of public and private contributions that joined in Bellevue a model of the community alliance required to synthesize that critical mass. Again, the first efforts were private. The BAM fund drive was launched in early 1997 and within five weeks $3 million had been garnered from East Side deep pockets, most importantly those of former Microsoft President Jon Shirley and his wife Mary. The Shirley's gift of $2 million lent even greater grace to the couple's reputation as the "patron saints of the region's arts scene." Within a week of this private accumulation the BAM campaign learned that the Bellevue City Council had agreed to offer assistance that was ambivalently described as "strong backing" and "less than was hoped for." Although univocal — the vote was 7 to 0 — the Council was still a bit skittish in its contributions to the BAM move and in the beginning gave a pledge for a mere $1.5 million. On March 19, 1997, the day following the vote, a *Seattle Times* editorial characterized it as "a deliberately cautious response [that] must be considered a worthwhile first step rather than an outright disappointment." The *Times*'s "first step" prediction was ultimately fulfilled and the total public contribution from the City of Bellevue to the building of BAM grew to $3 million.

Almost anything of size in Bellevue routinely involves and often begins with a consultation with the Kemper Freeman family. As the post–World War II developers of Bellevue Square, the Freemans played patron and host to the Bellevue Art Museum and its forebears, the Bellevue Arts and Crafts Fair and the Panaca Gallery since 1947. As a practical matter Johnson was not about to commit Foundation funds for the building of a new BAM without the Freeman family's cooperation in moving the museum out of the comfortable but less than ideal home it had occupied since 1983 in what one wag described as the "attic in the third floor of Bellevue Square." Don Johnson puts it directly: "In this special instance one needs to involve Kemper Freeman or forget it. We would never get it done without his cooperation."

Don Johnson's understanding of East Side politics and powers arose in part from his thirty-five-year residency in Bellevue. He had known and worked with Kemper Freeman, Sr. and Jr., since the '60s; both had been longtime clients of Bogle & Gates. Johnson agreed to lead a cadre of BAM campaigners in a visit with Kemper Freeman, Jr. The helpful trustee remembers, "We tiptoed into his office. Kemper was receptive. He said in effect, 'Well, yes, I think this is a good thing. You know when the kids get to be eighteen or so they have to fly the coop. I think it's time that the museum moved out.' So then we signed him up. He became chairman of the capital committee and has since given seven-figure gifts to the campaign." By midsummer of 1997 BAM fund-raising had reached $7 million. The following June Bill and Melinda Gates gave $1 million to the project. With this gift, the *Seattle Times* noted that "Bellevue Microsoft money has been very very good to the BAM, whose efforts to tap the region's high-tech wealth seem to be paying off handsomely." Johnson joined in with Foundation funds as well, initially giving $1 million in the early spring of 1998. That initial contribution grew to a total of $1.5 million for capital construction, with an additional $96,690 in other support. Ground-breaking for the new museum in the fall of 1999 featured some "audience participation performance art." On the building site—purchased for the museum by Jon and Mary Shirley—the footprint plan of the new three-story, 36,000-square-foot museum, designed by the internationally acclaimed architect Steven Holl, was outlined with fluorescent paint and guests were invited to take a "virtual tour" of the building. As part of the ritual groundbreaking, principal donors and players were given shovels embellished by local artists.

Although the building capital campaign was a complete success, BAM encountered start-up operational difficulties in its new and greatly expanded facilities. With its abrupt closing in the late summer of 2003, the Bellevue Art Museum was one of the more notable casualties of the regional recession. The inevitable soul searching followed. Attendance at the new location had very little of the serendipity connected with its first home in Bellevue

Square, the community's covered center for sidewalk traffic. The programs and exhibits themselves had to attract visits. And Bellevue as a city built on the mobility of the automobile found itself increasingly separated from Seattle not only by growing congestion on both sides of Lake Washington but also by the reluctance of a significant number of persons on the Seattle side — including art supporters — to cross the lake in order to visit even exciting new institutions on the East Side like the Bellevue Art Museum.

While disappointing, especially to Bellevue, the abrupt closing of BAM inspired a new group of community leaders to take a fresh look into the Museum's role and a shaping of its core and calling more in line with its earliest association with crafts. The temporarily darkened museum committed to this traditional aspect of its calling when it hired Michael W. Monroe as its new executive director and chief curator, and modified its name to Bellevue Arts Museum. Both the former curator-in-charge of the Renwick Gallery at the Smithsonian Institution and the former executive director of the American Craft Council, Monroe is a distinguished champion of crafts and is quoted at the head of the white paper on the Museum's new plans made public early in 2005. "Craft is a vital part of our heritage and stands as testimony to the undying value of works of hand, heart, and mind. Bellevue Arts Museum has the unique opportunity to become a regional center of national significance for craft. I look forward to this exciting challenge of making this museum's mission a reality." BAM reopened to the public on June 18, 2005, with four very well-received inaugural exhibitions, which according to Monroe "are marked by diversity of expression and approach to materials, symbols of the vast creative spirit that is the hallmark of contemporary craft and design." At this writing BAM has just completed its fifty-seventh Bellevue Arts and Crafts Fair, substantially breaking all prior attendance and art and craft sales records.

Johnson's first gift to the BAM initiative was leadership, not cash: piloting the entourage of Bellevue arts activists into the office of Kemper Freeman. The history of the Foundation has an activist side that sometimes found it making rescues, discovering deserving and otherwise neglected niches, and giving "momentum money" to get things going. The Olympic Sculpture Park is an example — a cherished one for Don Johnson — where "seed money" or "initiative money" was involved from the start.

At a sale price significantly reduced from its initial $23 million appraisal, Unocal proposed to deed a portion of its Seattle waterfront property north of Broad Street to the public-private forces gathered around the Seattle Art Museum, so long as the 8.5 acres remained open space. SAM envisioned a facility something like the Minneapolis Sculpture Garden that was built as an extension of the celebrated Walker Art Center and Guthrie Theater on an old armory site. By Johnson's reckoning it was "an opportunity of a lifetime." The parcel was "the last unimproved piece of land of significant size on Seattle's downtown waterfront that could be used for park or art purposes."

The deadline set for purchase lent an aura of real emergency to the entire campaign. With $16.5 million needed in five months, Don Johnson welcomed the first visit to the Foundation round table by a trio of effective suitors for SAM's Olympic Sculpture Park: Virginia Wright, Mimi Gates, and Brooks Ragen. Johnson quickly pledged $1 million. It was the Foundation's single largest grant to SAM in the nearly twenty years of its overall $4,763,673 support for the institution. As noted earlier, Johnson grew up and went to school near the area of the Park and its surrounding hills of Magnolia and Queen Anne, and confesses that these youthful associations helped him make a quick decision.

Olympic Sculpture Park on Seattle's waterfront, with proposed siting of "Eagle"

Both the size of the purchase price and the required rush to get it stimulated a good deal of debate among persons directly connected with Seattle Art Museum. Herman Sarkowsky, one of the city's prominent developer-philanthropists, was cool to the idea. He considered it poorly timed for a museum that was already struggling to increase its endowment. Johnson recalls a friendly discussion about the Sculpture Park project with Sarkowsky at a small fundraiser for the campaign held at the home of Bill Gates, Sr.

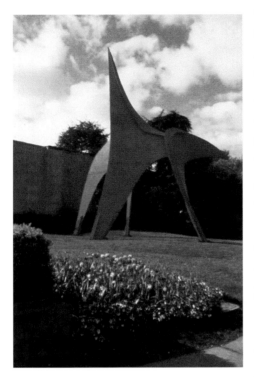

Alexander Calder's *Eagle*

" 'Herman,' I said, 'this is a one-time opportunity that we can't pass up.' He said, 'Well you know we have got to get that endowment.' I said, 'But Herman this is the only chance we will have.' 'Oh I know,' he said, 'but we have got to get the endowment.' " Inasmuch as Herman's wife Faye was serving as chair of SAM's endowment campaign his persistence was perhaps understandable. Johnson went on, "Ordinarily I would have not even tell the story, but Herman and Faye Sarkowsky have one of the longest and greatest records of philanthropy in this town and it is a good example of how persons of good intentions can differ." The campaign, of course, was a success, especially after former Microsoft President Jon Shirley and his wife, Mary, infused it with a sizable grant. Many months later Don Johnson encountered Brooks Ragen in downtown Seattle —Ragen had just come from a SAM board meeting—and asked him how the Sculpture Park was doing. Ragen answered, "Great. I told them at the meeting today that a hundred years from now it would be the Olympic Sculpture Park for which we would be remembered." The shared hope and expectation—"build the park and the sculpture will come"—is supported by Jon Shirley, who commented to *Seattle Times* reporter Florangela Davila,

"We collect sculpture and there really isn't a lot in downtown. We would like to feel that some of what we own, over time, will go to this garden."

Late in 2004, the Seattle Art Museum announced a "First Phase" for the Park that included an exhilarating list of acquisitions, donations, and loans. Included were works by Richard Serra, Cai Guo-Quiang, and Alexander Calder. Earlier, Jon and Mary Shirley had purchased Calder's thirty-nine-foot-tall *Eagle* (1971) for the Park, and the SAM announcement noted that the Shirleys were also loaning two sculptures from their private collection: Louise Nevelson's *Sky Landscape I* (1976) and Beverly Pepper's *Persephone Unbound* (1999). Announcing a "slated" opening for the Park in mid-2006, SAM's Deputy Director for Art Lisa Corrin explained, "The park's artistic program expands the definition of sculpture." An important part of this expansion was SAM's intent to "create a space for art that engages visitors of all ages and, additionally, raises awareness of the history and ecology of the park's site."

Several additional notable capital projects are described in *Legacy*. The projects and the chapters in which they are discussed are:

Part III

Other Beneficiaries

Part III of *Legacy* is rich with examples of the Foundation's great range of giving to support education at all levels, and to centers of all sorts — performance, cultural, heritage. This section of the book also brings to the fore a miscellany of worthy charges, including performances, exhibitions, individual works of art, and projects that needed some initial seeding or timely rescue. When considered together they may surely be imagined as that motif of giving, the cornucopia.

7 | Arts Education

University of Washington

As noted below, after the Cornish College of the Arts the list of Foundation gifts ranked by amount resumes with the Seattle Symphony. Thereafter it is all arts until the eleventh grantee: the University of Washington. And here is a rarity. Of the $2,505,263 granted to the university, a minority, or $1,080,263, went directly to arts. All of this (except for $30,263 designated in 1997 for the Meany Hall Art Campaign) was contributed in 2000, both for endowing a "Campaign for Arts" and for supporting the 2000 start-up of the first Summer Arts Festival, the principal expression of the Foundation-funded campaign. But how should the $150,000 granted to the on-campus Burke Museum for what is listed as its "Long-Term Exhibit Project" be classified? There is no easy accounting for what the relative arts-related and education-related value of this grant to the Burke might be, but the lesson of this ambiguity rests in the classical Horatian observation that we learn best what is artfully taught. This is, of course, also the fine arts pedagogy that we may discover and rediscover throughout this chronicle of the Kreielsheimer legacy.

An arts and education admixture is also expressed splendidly in the performance of the Henry Art Gallery. To that UW institution the Foundation gave $1,539,940, bringing its rank to number thirteen on the Foundation's list. If we join the sums given to the UW and to the Henry then the total for all UW-related projects ascends to a new station; they interpolate between number seven, the $4,565,600 given to ACT, and number eight, the $3,575,980 granted to the Corporate Council for the Arts, now known as ArtsFund. Charles Osborn's early Foundation gifts to the Henry were a mix of a few smaller endowment contributions and grants given for program and exhibition support — $270,000 in all. Johnson disbursed the rest, and, when compared, the amounts given to the Henry are a rough indication of the relative largess distributed by the two principal trustees over the life of the Foundation. Also, somewhat typically, the gifts by the second trustee were practically all for either the Gallery's endowment fund or for capital improvements to the plant itself.

The University of Washington was easily the biggest exception to the "private principal" when the Kreielsheimer Foundation was giving to educational institutions. In the opinion of many, including Don Johnson, the University of Washington is the most important institution in the state. The problem for Johnson was "how to give it an effective grant." Nothing was given to Washington State University, largely because of its remote location (for the Foundation) in Pullman. Closer to home, Western Washington University in Bellingham received $100,000 for its visual-arts program and another $3,000 for its music department. But in Seattle Johnson observes that while "the University is a thousand times larger than Cornish and is given millions, my attitude is that we have helped them both where they needed it." For a modern university disposed more toward technology and medicine, this need was most obviously in the arts. And, of course, this was also the need most appropriately engaged by Kreielsheimer. Don Johnson's admiration for the two UW presidents who held that post during the trustee's tenure also made it easier for him to give to the state school. Johnson thought Richard McCormick was the essence of eloquence and he describes Bill Gerberding as "a quiet but very astute man. He has a ton of integrity and has a community view of things." Thinking of Gerberding's part in Seattle Opera's capital campaign, Johnson concludes, "His name gave a project credibility to persons who do not have the time or inclination to study it. They figure if Gerberding is working for it, it must be okay."

Don Johnson approached Richard McCormick about how he might help the school's College of Arts and Sciences; and after some reflection with his brain trust, the president returned with the proposal for a Summer Arts Festival. Johnson assigned funds both to help it start up in the summer of 2000 and to endow its future. The Summer Arts Festival is resolutely multi-arts. Each year's Festival has been based on a theme: "Quartet" in 2000 and "Sphere" in its fourth year. Among the 2003 Festival offerings were a performance of Terry Riley's *Sun Rings* by the Kronos Quartet; a dance program on the influence of the circular form on choreographers, featuring the Simpson/Kyle Company and the UW-based Chamber Dance Company (its leader Hannah Wiley was also the festival's founding artistic director); a survey of experimental cinema classics by filmmaker Stan Brakhage; the play *Three Days of Rain*, by Richard Greenberg; a Meany Hall concert by the Seattle Repertory Jazz Orchestra; and three lectures on aesthetics, titled "Spherical Wisdom," by Ron Moore, an associate philosopher at the university. The running exhibitions — of artist James Turrell's *Skyspace* at the Henry Art Gallery and the *Out of Silence: The Enduring Power of Totem Poles* at the Burke Museum — were enclosed within the 2003 festival. In an interview by *Seattle Post-Intelligencer* music and dance critic R. M. Campbell, Festival Director Wiley noted, "The festival still allows you to challenge yourself at every level." She also confessed that it was becoming increasingly difficult to raise the extra money needed beyond that supplied by the dividends of the Kreielsheimer endowment. "We may have to make some hard choices in the future, but I am not letting myself think about that now. I want to bring this one to fruition and make it the very best." As it happened, however, the last festival was held in 2003, although as Michael Halleran, the divisional dean for Arts and Humanities noted, the Festival "gave shape to new connections, associations, and collaborations which have remained vital beyond [it]." Cuts in state funding to the school made it impossible to continue with the Festival itself. "New resources will be required if we are to produce it again, and we are hopeful that eventually such support will be forthcoming."

Don Johnson had second thoughts about an early inclination to use Foundation funds to endow an ethics program at the university involving the cooperation of the Law School, the School of Business, and the Jackson School of International Studies. "Frankly, I don't think a series of lectures is often all that effective, and in this case it might have been like preaching to the choir. The Kreielsheimer trustees could give grants in other areas legally so long as the predominant area was the arts. For instance, Charles Osborn made a couple of medical grants. But there was so much need in the arts that I was content to make them our focus. Ordinarily, the arts are last on the list, but not with Kreielsheimer." Consequently, one of the two $1 million grants to UW went to the Summer Arts Festival, and, of course in the larger sense, in support of the College of the Arts and Sciences.

The second million endows a university program that encourages excellence in primary and secondary education. The Kreielsheimer Fellowship is offered to two students in the College of Education's

Danforth Education Leadership Program, founded to create effective elementary and/or K-12 level principals in the Seattle Public Schools. The Kreielsheimer scholars get part-time pay plus tuition for the year with the program. Many of the program's graduates wind up as interns nearby the university on the Latona Campus of the Stanford International School, which is named for John Stanford, the late superintendent of Seattle Schools who promoted and operated on an inspirational formula he called "Love 'em and lead 'em." In its last year the Foundation also gave two smaller gifts to educators. The ARCS Foundation — for Achievement Rewards for College Scientists — received $10,000 for its work in supporting graduate education in the natural sciences, medicine, and engineering at the UW. An off-campus grant of $50,000 was given to the Alliance for Education's Thomas B. Foster Award for Program Excellence. Named for the late senior partner of the Foster Pepper & Shefelman law firm, the annual Foster Award is divided evenly between a top secondary school principal and her or his school.[*]

The Kreielsheimer Foundation also gave grants to the University of Washington Press and the school's Television Production services: $30,000 and $25,000 respectively. Another grant to the university sounds a personal note for the trustee. Moved by both sense and sentiment, Don Johnson embraced the opportunity to help out his alma mater, the UW School of Law. In the Foundation's eleventh hour he gave $250,000 for capital support to the new William H. Gates Hall. Although it was one of the few grants that were not in the Foundation's first area of concern, the arts, it was in the trustee's most familiar milieu. Johnson was a past president of the Board of Trustees of the Washington Law School Foundation and in 1999 he was also a member of the Dean's Advisory Committee on the UW Law School from which, as noted above, he graduated with the class of 1957.

Cornish College of the Arts

In its educational fold, the Cornish College of the Arts is the biggest Foundation story — both in the size of the grants and in the concerns of both trustees. Nellie Cornish was interested in "polishing all the corners" of

---

[*] Thomas B. Foster is also remembered for the development of his namesake house for homeless families.

her students. She said, "It has always been my belief that the musician should know something about dance, art, the theater, and literature . . . For example, if we had a violinist who was extremely talented but who was sloppy or too shy or nervous, we enrolled him in a dance, art, or theater class to correct the shortcoming." Well, perhaps. The idealistic piano teacher founded her namesake school in 1914 on Seattle's Capitol Hill. Just five years later she moved into the mildly Spanish landmark that sixty-six years later the Kreielsheimer Foundation would renovate, paying the entire cost of $1,524,099. Charles Osborn took such a hands-on attitude that he micromanaged the disbursement of payments to the variety of contractors who worked on the elaborate renovation.

During the school's golden years throughout the 1920s and into the Great Depression, Cornish was known both for its bohemian soirees and the extended parade down its halls of a distinguished band of artists. These included the composers Marcel Dupré and John Cage; the dancers Pavlova, Martha Graham, and Merce Cunningham; the painters Mark Tobey and Morris Graves, the writer Thornton Wilder, and the violinist Jacques Thibaud. Thereafter, whoever entered Kerry Hall was invited to feel their hallowed presence. The school's distinguished traditions made a pantheon of this big baroque box at the northwest corner of Roy and Harvard. It is this well-rounded and yet elite tradition in fine arts education that appealed to Charles Osborn, although he sometimes fretted about whether his Kreielsheimer scholars were going to live up to the school's promise — and theirs. The Foundation's Cornish files include a collection of student letters assuring the trustee that they are trying hard.

The initial 1985 description of the enduring Cornish scholarship program is very pointed about its links to the founders. Osborn intended to "make a viable scholarship program for artists of exceptional merit to advance recruitment and retention goals in each artistic discipline at Cornish in honor of the Kreielsheimer legacy. Students so favored are known as 'Kreielsheimer Scholars.' " Four years later, in a letter written to Cornish President Robert Funk, Osborn advises, "We expect Kreielsheimer Foundation sponsored graduates of the program will establish careers in the arts and that their talents will benefit others by way of example, teaching, composition, or performance. We are primarily interested in 'true artists' and less interested in those who go into the commercial art or design." Actually, for the practical purposes of giving scholarships the line Charles Osborn drew between fine and commercial arts was strict. He assumed that students of design might one day make a substantial income and yet get a free education with no obligation to return anything to the institution that gave it to them. And the students did receive. Each scholarship included tuition, books, supplies, and, if the winner did not reside in Seattle, a living allowance. In 1985, the scholarship program's first year, support for each student ranged from $6,100 to $10,000. (At the time the latter figure was greater than what many of the full-time Cornish faculty were making.) In Northwest high schools the competition for the awards was considerable. For the 1987–88 admissions to the class of 1991's four-year support, 175 students competed for five scholarships. Charles Osborn's commitment to the program was sealed in July 1992, days before his death. With a shaky signature he signed a letter to the Cornish president that confirmed his expectation that the "Foundation would permanently fund the program by creation of an endowment."

Weeks after Sergei P. Tschernisch arrived in the summer of 1994 he confessed to a local reporter, "Maybe it is true that one needs 'a bit of madness' to be president of Cornish College of the Arts." Like Robert Funk, his predecessor, Tschernisch needed the Kreielsheimer Foundation. Don Johnson, then finishing his second year as trustee, was ready to help. Generally, Johnson was faithful to a line of succession, furthering Foundation traditions inspired by the founder Leo Kreielsheimer and instituted by Charles Osborn. Any idea of doing otherwise was as distasteful to his sense of commitment as it was to his economic views. "I believed that I should not disrupt ongoing initiatives unless there was a compelling reason. It is wasteful. With Cornish I had confidence in what Charlie had started and I continued with it." Johnson also and almost instantly liked Tschernisch, the school's new larger-than-life president. Besides continuing Osborn's commitment to the scholarship program, Johnson purchased the three-story Century Terrace Apartments, directly to the west of Cornish for $594,144 in 1994, and three years later allotted another $146,802 to renovate the apartment building into the school's administrative offices. In 2003 the apartments and several other Cornish structures contiguous to Kerry Hall were, with Johnson's approval, sold to provide capital that helped fund the school's expansion to its new Denny Triangle campus.

Also in 1994 under Tschernisch's leadership and with help from Kreielsheimer, the school began making plans. The president announced that "Cornish will be looking at a major campaign in 1995 . . . Our art department turns students away now. They desperately need new facilities. We have almost no choice but to build." While acknowledging that it would be a tough campaign, Tschernisch also exhibited the kind of zest required to mount it. "Cornish hasn't entered into the fray for a long time. It's about time." While preparing his forces, the president turned to Johnson, the trusted trustee, who responded, "We think it is important to strengthen the ability of Cornish to provide arts education to the Pacific Northwest region. . . . The Foundation has been working with the school to fund studies, including a long-range plan for a gradual and efficient expansion." Appropriate to the contemporary concern for community Uncle Sergei's emphasis was different than Aunt Nellie's philosophy of the "complete artist." Tschernisch taught, "At this point in American history we desperately need to train artists to work in society. The arts confront reality, they make us wiser, they give us hope. All great cities are remembered for their culture, not their politics or their economy. I would love to see Cornish as an important part in the Seattle arts community, a vital part of this mixture."

In the summer of 1997, Kreielsheimer co-trustees Gus Cleveland (representing SeaFirst Bank) and Don Johnson, with Sandy Fry, Johnson's assistant, met with Sergei Tschernisch, Cornish trustees Eve and Chap Alvord, and the school's director of operations and facilities, Vicki Clayton, to review accomplishments and assess plans. In the three years since president Tschernisch's arrival the college had operated in the black, and a campus plan had been constructed. Reviews of the curriculum, the faculty, the board of trustees, and the school's business development had also been concluded. This generally sanguine report may be compared to one issued twenty years earlier by the Northwest Association of Schools and Colleges in its review of the school's successful attempt at accreditation. The reviewers found that "crowded and obsolete facilities are the chief bar to any further development of this institution. Immediate planning and funding must begin to resolve this limitation — which once a quaint cause for pride in terms of 'success in the face of adversity' — now threatens the very existence of the school. The board and the president (then Melvin Strauss) must address this problem without delay."

Although matters had changed considerably in the two decades since accreditation, they had in at least one respect stayed the same. Not surprisingly, the 1997 Campus Plan concluded that the school needed to add a new and larger campus while still holding on to its heritage at Kerry Hall. Numerous buildings in various locations were evaluated and it was determined that the South Lake Union area — then still called the "Seattle Commons" from efforts in the early 1990s to transform the neighborhood into a verdant urban village — best met the needs of the school. The most important part of this choice was, no doubt, the decision of the neighborhood's biggest landlord, the Paul Allen Foundation, to donate two blocks within the Commons to Cornish, provided the venerable school demonstrated that it could raise the money to do the rest.

The new campus is the centerpiece of the overall $73.9 million capital campaign that also includes strengthening of the endowment, enhancing the faculty support fund, and building resources for special academic projects. The Main Campus Center was completed in the summer of 2003 and celebrated that September with a festive ribbon-cutting ceremony. Next, the historic Sons of Norway Hall (renamed the Raisbeck Performance Hall) and the Orion Center were added to the new campus. When complete, the expanded and consolidated campus will double the space available for arts education and performance, from the 113,000 square feet offered on the old campus on Capitol Hill to about 225,000 on the new campus in the Denny Triangle.

For its part the Foundation continued, as promised, to support the Kreielsheimer Scholarship program, to which it had given nearly $4 million over the fifteen years since the program began in the 1985–86 term. Now the scholarships were divided into two lines. A Classic Program extended the original plan of four years' tuition with stipends for books, supplies, and living expenses through the year 2003–04. The new Dynamic Program was launched in the academic year 2001–02 and designed to attract first-year students by providing half-tuition grants that were conditionally renewable through a second year.

The number of new scholarships that might be offered depended upon the payout of the $3 million endowment given by the Foundation for the program. In 2000 this was still kept with the Kreielsheimer Remainder Foundation until the school formed its own foundation with the special function of managing the endowment according to its rules. One of the prescriptions was that students granted scholarships through this fund continue to be recognized as Kreielsheimer Scholars and that, through an alumni relations program, the college endeavor to maintain contact with them "as a demonstration" — to quote the terms of the endowment — "of the effectiveness of the program in supporting artists of promise early in their careers." This interest in tracking is in part also a call for gratitude toward the Kreielsheimer legacy. It acts as a kind of small but repeated reminder that such beneficence as the $11-plus million given to Cornish began with the generous imaginations of Leo and Greye Kreielsheimer, administered through the discernment of first Charles Osborn and finally Don Johnson. Such admiration is one of the core civic virtues. Appropriately, in 1991, Charles F. Osborn was awarded an honorary Doctor of Fine Arts from the unique arts school founded on Seattle's Capitol Hill; Don Johnson was similarly honored on May 13, 2000.

Independent Colleges

Arts and education are the two pillars upon which the Kreielsheimer Foundation was built. A large percentage of Foundation gifts sent north to Alaska landed in schools or cultural centers because, unlike the Puget Sound region, the forty-ninth state has few large arts organizations to accept sizable gifts. A great majority of the Foundation's giving stayed within fifty miles of Seattle Center, and most of this went directly to the arts. About one-fifth of the total $100 million plus disbursed by the Foundation went to schools or other institutions for educational purposes. It would, however, be a mistake to conclude thereby that gifts for education were one-fifth the amount of the former. In truth the accumulated sum given to all schools and centers for projects not involving the arts was considerably smaller. Arts education was the target of the greatest percentage of funds directed to education. The evidence for this is readily apparent. Slightly more than half of the nearly $20 million given for education went to one institution with art in its name: the Cornish College of the Arts. In total disbursements, Cornish was third on the list of recipients, gaining a total of $11,086,338 from Kreielsheimer. The Seattle Symphony Orchestra is listed immediately after the school with accumulated Foundation gifts of $10,743,867. Immediately before Cornish the largest to the Seattle Opera of $11,209,803 amounted to only a little more than that given the school. The biggest gift, of course, came to the City of Seattle: $18,948,271, with $10 million of this given as catalyst for the transformation of the Opera House into the Marion Oliver McCaw Hall and the funding of the Kreielsheimer Promenade in its forecourt. That Seattle Center was at the center of the Kreielsheimer universe is revealed also in this: practically all of the nearly $19 million given to the city went for projects on the Center, or contiguous to it, along Mercer Street—including the K block.

The trustee's freedoms within the Foundation's art-oriented guidelines certainly inclined the Irish-Catholic in Charles Osborn in the direction of his own affections when he gave early aid to both Gonzaga and Seattle Universities. Don Johnson speculates that while Osborn's client and friend, Leo Kreielsheimer, might have found these sentimental links amusing, they were also appropriate. While the Foundation excluded giving grants to religious organizations per se, it did not restrict funding them for arts-oriented projects. Johnson explains, "It would not have been cricket to give these same schools contributions for the 'bishop's fund,' but in all instances Charles Osborn used the Foundation's 'arts clause.' Charles made some early grants to Gonzaga. I, however, did not give any more because the school was in Spokane and that was beyond our Western Washington area." Still, by Osborn's doing, Gonzaga received a total of $1,250,000. With part of this the school endowed a Kreielsheimer Chair in the Arts Department and a Kreielsheimer Visiting Artists Program. A half million dollars was used as capital support for the school's Center for Visual Art.

When the Foundation gave to educational institutions it was most often to private schools, primarily because they enjoyed no security in tax revenues. For instance, $50,000 was granted to Whitman College and $25,000 to Seattle Pacific University. The Pilchuck Glass School, a private institution dedicated to making art from glass, received a sizable offering of $422,860, a combination of capital and endowment support. An early and small exception to the "private principal" was Charles Osborn's gift of $2,000 in the mid-1980s to support a "Visual Arts Exhibit" at Evergreen State College in Olympia. By comparison, Don Johnson returned to

Olympia—or near, it to Lacey—in 1988 and ultimately gave $500,000 to Saint Martin's College (now St. Martin's University) for what the Foundation spreadsheet lists as "educational purposes" but which were still arts related.

Saint Martin's was, in Johnson's own humorous allusion to Osborn's gifts to Gonzaga and Seattle University, "my Catholic institution." He grew attached to it. "I worked with them as their attorney quite a bit in the 1980s, and I knew how impecunious they were and what fine people they were as well. We matched a grant from a friend, Tom O'Grady, who was a wonderful philanthropist. He was an Irish Catholic who had attended Saint Martin's and had gone on to make a lot of money in New York. The school planned to put up Quonset huts for their arts center, but Tom and I challenged each other—so we each put up a $250,000 (for $500,000 total) for a permanent building that will be good for 50 or a 100 years. I am amazed how substantial it is." Housing arts-education classes as well as both teaching and rehearsal space for the theater arts and music programs, the school's new Kreielsheimer Hall Arts Center was also an exception to the Foundation's general experience of having other names attached to projects to which they gave large and early capital grants. This time Tom O'Grady took the initiative and instructed that his name not be used. The alum made other gifts to Saint Martin's, and early in 2001 the O'Grady Library opened on campus. After O'Grady was lost to a heart attack, Don Johnson gave another grant to Saint Martin's in his friend's honor.

Independent Schools K-12

Of all the K-through-12 schools that received help, Epiphany School may have the closest personal ties to the Foundation. The Kreielsheimer family was connected with the school when Olivia Kreielsheimer's daughter, Courtenay Berry, was a student at Epiphany. For Don Johnson, the ties extended through one of Seattle's more energetic arts advocates, James Tune. A close friend of Johnson's, as well as a managing partner of Johnson's firm Bogle & Gates, Tune was an Epiphany parent. Another link was Chap Alvord, an Epiphany parent as well as a school trustee and, with his wife Eve, another of Seattle's activist patrons admired by Johnson. A total of $162,500 was given to Epiphany, beginning with a grant of $2,500 for the purchase of computers. (This gift was made in 1983, about the time many of us were first being introduced to the personal computer. As already noted, the Foundation gave another early computer-conversion grant to the Seattle Symphony in 1982.) A second gift to Epiphany from Charles Osborn came in 1985: $10,000 for a fine-arts program that helped established the school's music program. During the 1997 capital campaign for construction of the school's art studio the Foundation gave gifts of $35,000 and $65,000. Finally, Epiphany School was one of the many institutions that were refreshed in the generous outpouring of the Foundation's last year, when it received another $50,000 for its arts enrichment endowment.

Northwest School, another Kreielsheimer beneficiary, meets in the classic "box design" Seattle Public School that, when it opened in 1905, was named Summit School. It faces Summit Avenue north of Union Street and straddles the soft border between Seattle's First and Capitol hills. By the mid-1960s too few children were living in the immediate neighborhood to keep Summit open. In 1980 Northwest School moved in. In its third year the school asked for and received, through Charles Osborn, a grant for $10,000 to equip a ceramics studio. In 1986 another $10,000 was added to help with the school's fine-arts complex. The largest and last grant came in 2000 through Don Johnson — $100,000 for the school's orchestra endowment. The advanced musicianship at Northwest School is impressively expressed in musical theater, the school's chorus, its jazz ensemble, and its chamber orchestra. The orchestra has toured Europe, Asia, and Cuba, and has released its first compact disc. Northwest student and now teacher Oceania Eagan may be considered a poster child for the Foundation. Graduating from Northwest School, she went on to Cornish College of the Arts as a Kreielsheimer Scholar. After earning her BFA she returned to Northwest School as an arts instructor.

Forest Ridge, like Summit originally a Capitol Hill school dating from the early twentieth century, moved in 1971 to its nineteen-acre campus on Bellevue's Somerset Hill overlooking Lake Washington. The Catholic girls school can claim that one hundred percent of its students have laptops and also go on to college. As an apt example, Ammine Berry, Leo and Greye Kreielsheimer's granddaughter, matriculated from Forest Ridge in 1984 and continued on to college. Forest Ridge received $40,000 from the Foundation.

In 1996 Zion Preparatory Academy moved from St. Marie's Church where it was founded in 1982 to its present quarters in Seattle's Rainier Valley. Zion first received a gift of $10,000 from the Foundation for the development of its arts program. In its last year the Foundation gave another $150,000 toward the school's campaign to extensively remodel its plant, which was formerly a medical recovery center. (In 2002–03 all tuitions for the approximately 350 students at Zion were subsidized, and ninety-seven percent of the student body that year was African American.)

Also in 2000, the Foundation contributed $50,000 to the Seattle Academy to help complete the Arts Center for its opening in 2001. Among the amenities of Arts Center are a 250-seat theater, a darkroom, a video production studio, and several classrooms for music instruction and practice, one of which is fronted with a plaque that thanks the Foundation.

The $100,000 Kreielsheimer contributed to Overlake School's $8.5 million capital campaign was part of the critical mass that created what has become a venue for the greater East Side. The new arts complex, with its Arts Barn (the visual arts building) and the Fulton Performing Arts Center opened in 2001. The performing arts center includes a 350-seat, fully rigged theater, a black-box combined theater and drama classroom, choral and instrumental music rooms, a practice room, and a lobby that also serves as a student gallery. This Redmond location was chosen by the Seattle Chamber Music Festival to schedule several performances during August 2005, in addition to its Lakeside summer concerts in July, and likewise by the Seattle Youth Symphony Orchestra as one of the two summer venues for its Marrowstone-in-the-City day program for students aged thirteen to twenty-three. As Mike James notes in chapter 1 on the Foundation's part in the musical arts, Kreielsheimer also gave to the SYSO.

The Foundation helped the University Preparatory Academy in north Seattle with a $50,000 donation toward its capital construction project in 2000. The completion of the Hooper Fine Arts Center in the spring of 2002 was one of several physical improvements to the school that were the result of the campaign.

Three traditional stalwarts of private education hereabouts also received gifts from the Foundation. In 1986 Charles Osborn contributed $25,000 to Annie Wright School in Tacoma to help endow a chair for the performing arts, and in 2000 Johnson added another $25,000 for uses connected with the school's Kemper Center Theatre. Between 1985 and 2000, Bush School received $150,000 from Kreielsheimer for general support, capital funds, and the school's endowment. Bush School is Washington State's oldest independent K-12 institution and is located in Seattle's Madison Valley neighborhood a few blocks from the Denny Blaine neighborhood home where it began with six students in 1924. The student body now numbers 500. Lakeside School at Seattle's northern city limits was granted $100,000 for its 1999 Now Campaign, which included the construction of two new buildings.

Finally, making three exceptions to the Foundation's general interest in independent schools over public ones, are its grants in support of traveling musicians in public schools. First, Charles Osborn made a $25,000 contribution in 1986 to the Seattle School District for the All-City Band's trip to Washington, D.C. Then, in 2000, $8,000 went to Chief Sealth High School to help pay for the performance of its Honor Choir at Carnegie Hall in New York City. And Garfield High received two grants for its traveling orchestra — $10,000 in 1997 for a trip to the International Youth and Music Festival, and $7,500 in 2000 for its performances that summer in Japan.

Interest in Youth

The Kreielsheimer legacy is enlivened by its gifts that have served youth not only through schools but other institutions as well. As a foundation with a primary interest in the arts, Kreielsheimer most often sent its funds to organizations concerned with youth for arts-related projects — but not always. The first youth-oriented grant, sent in 1981 — the Foundation's first annum of gift giving — was the $20,000 boon to help establish the Northwest School for Hearing Impaired Children. The following year Charles Osborn continued in this line with a grant for the Child Hearing League but then also dispensed a $5,000 gift to the Northwest Boys Choir (for office equipment, not voice lessons). In 1983, the Foundation helped what has been historically one of the region's most popular charities, the Children's Orthopedic Hospital, with a grant not for art but, again, for equipment. Osborn returned to Children's in 1985, committing $20,000 for the hospital's program for diabetes education. However, beginning in 1985, the great majority of new youth-oriented gifts from the Foundation were to arts institutions. That year the Seattle Young Artists Music Festival received a $5,000 gift; the Seattle Youth Symphony Orchestra got its first Kreielsheimer aid, $5,000 for "general support"; and the Seattle Children's Theatre also got its first small grant from the Foundation. A precise $2,465 was donated for Theatre-In-Sign, a three-year pilot project produced jointly by the Children's Theatre and the Hearing Impaired Arts Program. The letter requesting the grant explained that "there are approximately twenty thousand deaf and hearing-impaired individuals in King County. 'Theater-In-Sign' is the only program of its kind in Western Washington for this special population." Charles Osborn turned his youth-oriented giving to Seattle Center in 1987 with an early gift for the then-new Children's Museum, an institution that Don Johnson would revisit again in 1995 and every year through 1999, giving $50,000 in all to the Museum's capital campaign.

In 1987 Osborn supported music appreciation for young people by giving $5,000 to the Northwest Chamber Orchestra for its Youth Concert Program. The following year he gave directly to young players with renewed support for the Seattle Youth Symphony through a gift of $10,000 to its Marrowstone-in-the-City music festival. Ultimately, $347,860 was given to the Seattle Youth Symphony and all but $15,000 of it was from the hands of Don Johnson.

Both the relative balanced weight of giving and the continuity of grantees between the two trustees were, as noted earlier, commonplace in the Foundation's practices. In frequently giving the greatest largess to institutions first benefited by Osborn with modest grants, Johnson created and conserved Foundation traditions and thereby also honored the first trustee's choices. As for the Youth Symphony and arts for youth generally, Don Johnson is clear on why he gave Foundation support. "We have got to start people young in the arts. We have a lot better chance if we excite their brains before they leave their teen years. For instance, there are a lot of capable artists and performers who were without meaningful ambition or goals until they got into a high school stage play or musical group that they enjoyed, and the experience changed their lives for the better. That is what a good theater or music or arts teacher can do in a high school."

The last grant to the Youth Symphony was $250,000, which Johnson gave to establish the Vilem Sokol Endowment Fund "in commemoration of the many years of devoted service to the Seattle Youth Symphony Orchestra by Vilem Sokol." Sokol had recently retired after many years as the music director of the Youth Symphony. Don Johnson first encountered Sokol in his position as a young music professor at the University of Washington in 1951. The business and pre-law major needed an elective class and attempted to enroll in a music appreciation class given by a professor who had a reputation of giving "easy As." After learning that the class was filled, Johnson was asked if he would be interested in another class on the same subject offered by a young professor, Vilem Sokol. Johnson enrolled and to his delight found Sokol to be one of the most inspiring teachers he had ever encountered, stirring Johnson's incipient interest in classical music. Soon the future Kreielsheimer trustee was deeply enamored by the likes of Beethoven, Brahms, Richard Strauss, Stravinsky, and Debussy. Johnson remembers fondly an after-class discussion he had with the professor. Then a mere twenty-one, Johnson was a fan of the Stan Kenton "progressive jazz" band, which featured a loud brass section capable of considerable tonal dissonance. Kenton's sidemen, including saxophonist Bud Shank (who would later became a teacher both at the Olympic Music Festival at Port Townsend and at Cornish) regularly won the annual "best" awards of *Downbeat* magazine. Johnson mustered the courage after class one day to ask the professor whether Kenton might be leading in new musical techniques of interest to the classical composers. Johnson recalls, "Sokol in response looked at me in a kindly, patient, but paternal way and gently said, in effect, 'Don, Igor Stravinsky, Bela Bartok, and others have been using such dissonance techniques with brass instruments since the early part of the century.' " Johnson was appropriately impressed and notes that while he hasn't played a Kenton record in years he regularly enjoys Stravinsky.

Exciting the artistic potential of adolescents is also the annual focal point of the Seattle Center Academy. Since it began in 1991 with a Kreielsheimer seed grant, this two-week summer program continues to bring Seattle middle school boys and girls together with local artists — many of them from mainstay Seattle Center institutions like the Children's Theatre and the Pacific Northwest Ballet — for an intense immersion in practically all the arts. At the end of each term student work is shown, both in exhibition and on stage with a grand finale. The August 8, 2003, performance involved a majority of the school's roughly 300 students making art—dance, theater, music, poetry, and fashion—on the stage of the Bagley Wright Theatre, the venue packed with friends, parents, and the students themselves. Don Johnson, who notes that from the beginning of his trusteeship he "wouldn't miss it," was in attendance at the frequently jumping theater.

The idea for this summer school was Seattle Center Director Virginia Anderson's, although when she first visited Charles Osborn to ask for support she recalls, "I didn't even have a written proposal." But Anderson remembers that the trustee "saw it" and was "instantly enthusiastic." Osborn explained to the director, "I have been trying to convince Cornish to do this for a long time. Let's just do it." He and Anderson agreed that the school should draw on kids from all income groups throughout King County and that there "be no line drawn between the kids who lived on waterfront property and those who lived in a homeless shelter." Osborn soon gave the Seattle Center Foundation $50,000 to study and assemble the Academy. Anderson said, "That was a proud moment—for you know, Charles could be pretty gruff. Focus groups told us first that the kids that needed it most were from middle school. The second thing they told us was that we would not want to work with those kids because it is the hardest age group. So we decided that that was our challenge—those were the kids we should serve. With Kreielsheimer help we made it happen in nine months. Since 1994 we have fully integrated severely disabled children— kids that range from Down syndrome to pretty significant cerebral palsy. Students from previous academies volunteer as their mentors and spend the whole day with them. It is one of those things in life that sort of makes it all real." The Foundation awarded a total of $660,000 to the Academy through the Seattle Center Foundation, the nonprofit corporation established in 1977 to encourage such giving for a variety of projects on the Seattle Center campus.

8 | Seattle Center:
The City of Seattle

The tradition for using the Seattle Center site for culture and performance began with the Duwamish Indians. David and Louisa Denny chose the site for their donation claim in the early 1850s. Long before then, this lowland meadow, lying between Denny and Queen Anne Hills, had been used perennially by the Indians for Potlatch, the North Coast native ritual of gift-giving. The Denny family supplied much of the pioneer community's produce with vegetables from the large garden they planted on the rich swale near the contemporary footprints of the Intiman Theatre, the Phelps Center, and McCaw Hall—all beneficiaries of the Kreielsheimer Foundation. Following the gift of the greater portion of the Denny garden tracts to the city in 1889 for "public use forever," the future Seattle Center became one of the community's favorite fields for organized baseball and visiting circuses.

In 1927 the voters passed a $900,000 bond issue to develop the Denny gift with a Civic Auditorium. The kernel for this construction had been planted nearly a half century earlier when James Osborne, a local saloonkeeper, died without heirs and, hoping to better himself posthumously, left much of his fortune to the city for a public hall. James Osborne made his fortune in the sale of spirits, as the Kreielsheimer brothers had, although Osborne did it one bottle at a time. By 1927 Osborne's $22,000—in 1881 a sum comparable to the city budget—had swelled to $120,000, a tidy start for the auditorium that in another thirty-five years was redressed to become the Opera House for Century 21.

For many years after it was created from the improvements left by the 1962 World's Fair, Seattle Center had to struggle with the recurring notion that both it and the lower Queen Anne neighborhood that surrounds it were either wearing out, or, worse, down and out. In truth, it depended upon where one looked. While parts of Seattle Center were extraordinarily busy—like the Opera House—others were dormant. The Kreielsheimer

Foundation was a great player in helping ameliorate public ambivalence by making many contributions to the vitality of Seattle Center and most of the arts organizations it hosts. For example, the proposal to build a new Children's Theatre — ironically on the moribund site of Century 21's "House of Tomorrow" exhibit — was treated cautiously by a philanthropic establishment that, in the early 1990s, remembered the leaks and litigation that followed the flawed construction of the Bagley Wright Theatre in 1983. Seattle Center Director Virginia Anderson recalls that the Center's unhappy experience with the Bagley Wright Theatre was "a bad mark to overcome . . . so for the Kreielsheimer Foundation to have come forward and demonstrate early trust in the Children's Theater project was a big deal."

When all $100-plus million of the Foundation's giving is sorted out, about half of it was disbursed to the Seattle Center and its several resident institutions.* If there is a lesson in this commitment, it is, at least in part, this: In spite of the reversals, Charles Osborn's enthusiasm for the K block was the early touchstone for the Foundation's lavish commitment to enlarging the legacy of Potlatch Meadows.

* For more information, see also chapter 22.

9 | ArtsFund/Corporate Council for the Arts

After a period when it used two names — as the Corporate Council for the Arts and the Arts Fund — in 2003 the institution responsible for giving prudent order to so much regional giving to the arts became simply ArtsFund. The new name is more descriptive of the wide range of sources, including many individual donors, from which ArtsFund was then increasingly beginning to draw its support.

Founded in 1969 as the United Arts Council and renamed in 1974 the Corporate Council for the Arts (CCA), it was designed to centralize much of the giving to nonprofit arts organizations in King and Pierce counties while ensuring that the grants are made fairly. ArtsFund oversees corporate and individual giving to the arts, and about a thousand area businesses and individuals donate both time and money to the process. In 2002 more than $2.7 million was granted to sixty-five arts groups, although all but $300,000 of this was used for sustaining grants to large institutions like the Seattle Symphony. Peter F. Donnelly has been president of ArtsFund since 1989. He started his career in arts management as an intern with the Repertory Theatre soon after its founding following the 1962 Century 21 Exposition. Through the combination of his robust intelligence and engaging garrulity, Donnelly became both the theater's producing director and a spirited force in triggering the momentum to build the Bagley Wright Theatre and see it open in 1983. While at the Rep, the quick-study Donnelly soon became a veteran at nourishing the local arts scene with donations mostly from Seattle businesses.

Once the mantle of trustee was laid upon his shoulders Don Johnson was fortunate to have Peter Donnelly to consult. It was highly desirable for Johnson and Donnelly, as leaders of foundations with similar calls, to work well together, and they did. By Johnson's description, "For the overall arts scene, Peter is more knowledgeable than anyone else in town, and he also has the big picture." Donnelly's description of Don Johnson is also gener-

Peter Donnelly, executive director of the Corporate Council for the Arts and ArtsFund from 1987 to 2005

ous. "Don learned very quickly. He took to his new role with the zest and curiosity that is demanded by the arts." Eventually the savvy advice that the experienced Donnelly directed toward the Foundation was returned with generous support and ultimately a home for ArtsFund in the Century Building.

After Johnson formally retired from Bogle & Gates in 1995 at age sixty-five, he continued to find a home for himself and the Foundation with the 108-year-old law firm until its surprising close in 1999, when the Foundation and its trustee had sixty days to make other arrangements. Fortunately for the Foundation, deciding where to relocate was both easy and fitting. The Century Building, on Harrison Street a mere block from Seattle Center, was not only located out of the high-priced downtown, it was also owned by the Foundation. Within a year of settling into third-floor offices of the four-story building, Don Johnson made decisions that would transform the Century Building into a center for community arts, and one that would carry on long after the Kreielsheimer Foundation closed in the late summer of 2000.

Don Johnson's links with the Century Building predated his trusteeship. "It is one of the oldest stories of Leo Kreielsheimer, Charlie Osborn, and myself. After he sold his canneries in the early 1960s Leo became a retired entrepreneur. Charlie was his estate attorney, and I did a lot of real estate and property management for Leo, and the Century Building was an example of the kind of investing that he was making in the late '60s and early '70s. Of course when I helped him buy it I never in my wildest dreams imagined the history the building would have when carried forward. At first Seattle-First National Bank was the key tenant on the main level. After Martin Selig lured SeaFirst into one of his new buildings nearby

The Century Building, home of ArtsFund and King FM

and paid the balance of the SeaFirst lease, we brought in other tenants. When Leo died the building stayed in the estate and remained there as well following Greye's death in 1980. The building was then distributed under the terms of the Kreielsheimer will to its namesake foundation. The Foundation's assets were not mainly in real estate but rather in securities, and stocks and cash accounts and such. I tried to sell the Century Building in the mid-1990s because at the time we did not want to be in the business of giving away real estate to arts groups per se. I got a conditional offer from a well-known contractor in Seattle but when they later returned with a substantially lowered offer I concluded that we could do better things with the building than sell it at a very reduced price. About one year later, when the real estate market was booming, the CCA/ArtsFund lost its rent-free space downtown and was given only thirty days to move out. I told Peter Donnelly that if he and his board could not find another place, to consider coming out to the Century Building, for after all it was only a block from Seattle Center and about five minutes from downtown. Well, they came — and right away we gave them a virtually rent-free term from 1997 to 2000. Although in the beginning I was not sure that it would necessarily be the right fit, it worked out so well that I decided to give the building to them—but with the understanding that it would be used both for their headquarters and as an arts center. A footnote to this story is that a year or two later KING FM, which had earlier been given by the Bullitt sisters and family in equal shares to the Seattle Symphony, Seattle Opera, and the CCA/ArtsFund, also had to move. Patsy Collins liked the concept of putting KING FM in the Century Building and in my opinion the station made a beautiful addition at the ground level when they moved in. It is street-friendly now, and you can see it when you drive by—it has a certain class. The classical music station also pays rent, although it is a low rent that is of course ultimately redistributed back to the arts—to the Seattle Opera, the Seattle Symphony, and to ArtsFund. Well, the Century Building story is a wonderful story—Peter has told me so many times. If you can't pay your staff as much as you would like at least it is a fine place to be in and nothing like being stuffed in a mini-room or behind a partition somewhere in a warehouse."

The gift of the $2 million building was announced in April 1999. The following spring at its annual luncheon in the Westin Hotel Grand Ballroom, the CCA/ArtsFund's annual report to more than a thousand leaders in business and the arts included giving the Outstanding Foundation Leadership in the Arts award to the Kreielsheimer Foundation for its years of service to regional arts. A few months later the Foundation included among its last grants $1 million for the ArtsFund endowment, and in turn ArtsFund named the endowment the Kreielsheimer Fund. It was the second million given by the Foundation to the nonprofit. The first came cumulatively through annual grants that were first made in 1993. Late in 2000 Peter Donnelly noted that the new Kreielsheimer Fund, when combined with the lease revenues expected from the Century Building, would generate about $150,000 a year for ArtsFund. Less than two years later, at its 14th Annual Corporate Council Celebrates the Arts Luncheon, Donnelly calculated that since its founding in 1969 the ArtsFund annual funds had gathered and distributed $44 million for regional arts organizations and another $4.5 million for its endowment programs. Donnelly's statistics were meant in part as a palliative for the general malaise felt following the terrorist attacks of September 11 and a local economy gone quickly sour.

10 | Regional Performance, Heritage, and Cultural Centers

With a few exceptions, community-supported orchestras construct seasons that are well-stocked with classical examples of "oldies but goodies." The rare concert performance of a Janáček or Hanson opera will count as an experiment for most symphonies. But the range of arts and culture in any city of size is always much greater than the sum of its big five — the symphony, opera, ballet, visual art, and theater — no matter how far they extend their programming beyond Mozart, Beethoven, Verdi, Puccini, Wagner, Tchaikovsky, Shakespeare, and other masters. The Kreielsheimer Foundation, of course, gave to a great variety of presenters well beyond these established stalwarts. This second list is longer, and includes community performance centers, and museums of many sorts. And the Foundation also gave to one floating heritage landmark: The *Virginia V*, the last of Puget Sound's once extensive Mosquito Fleet.

The relatively recent rise of community theaters and performance centers throughout Washington State offers some of the best evidence for the frequent claim that the late twentieth century was stirred by something resembling an arts renaissance. The Kreielsheimer Foundation played its part by supporting an array of Puget Sound–based performing-arts facilities that promote the general building of community through diverse presentations and sometimes direct arts training as well. Those venues that benefited by Foundation gifts were generally nonprofit institutions and not Seattle's grander commercial presenters like the Paramount and 5th Avenue theaters. Yet while not in the main focus of Foundation funding, these particular groups are also important contributors to local culture.

The Foundation gave a number of grants to help strengthen the network of community theaters and performance centers around Puget Sound. Don Johnson observed, "Everyone cannot go to the queen city of Seattle, but if there is a theater presenting quality performances in their own communities, they can get there. For instance, we supported theaters in Bremerton, Bellingham, and Olympia, and performance centers in Renton and Kirkland. This last, the Kirkland Performance Center, is a heroic project to which we gave a relatively modest grant — intending, for instance, to bring the Pacific Northwest Ballet or the Empty Space Theater over to the East Side. We wanted to give parents in Redmond the chance to take their kids into Kirkland for a performance when they couldn't or wouldn't come all the way into Seattle. This arrangement would both strengthen the Empty Space Theater — or any other group traveling to the center — and also open new opportunities to the artists on the East Side."

Once the Kirkland Performance Center opened in June 1998, it soon fulfilled the vision described for it by both its founders and admired by the Foundation. The inaugural season featured performances by the Northwest Chamber Orchestra, Village Theater, Pacific Northwest Ballet, the Seattle Children's Theatre, and many others. The Foundation helped stimulate the fund-raising in mid-September 1994 when it announced a $100,000 challenge grant engineered so that one dollar would be given for every two dollars raised in gifts exceeding $5,000. To add excitement, a deadline was set: the year's end. As Steven Lerian, the Center's executive director, notes, "The Kreielsheimer Foundation took a leadership role in providing the spark that ignited the community to rally behind the project. . . . The willingness to comprehend the big picture of this project and the community's will to see it completed was typical of the Kreielsheimer history of making impact grants to arts organizations across the region." Originally the Foundation had contemplated a $50,000 grant, but agreed to increase it if the facility was increased from 300 seats to 400 seats. All told, the Foundation gave more than $300,000 to this new East Side venue that featured 402 seats arranged in a steep rake of thirteen rows, putting the farthest seat only forty feet from the stage. The Kirkland Performance Center is rarely dark. Typically, its year-round season features more than 250 performances.

The first of the seven grants directed to the Admiral Theatre in Bremerton was for a Seattle Symphony performance on April 3, 1998. The Symphony returned again in both 1999 and 2000. The last appearance was billed by the theater as a "sumptuous evening of fine food, friends, and the music of twentieth-century composers" featuring "the glorious sound of this world-class orchestra." Performances at the Admiral by the Spectrum

Dance Theatre and the Seattle Opera Young Artists were also subsidized by the Foundation. The Foundation gave a total of $152,500 to the Admiral; the last—an "unrestricted grant" dated July 25, 2000—was for $50,000, at the time a typical figure for the Foundation's largess as it approached the term deadline prescribed by Leo Kreielsheimer a quarter-century earlier.

Several lesser grants to community venues illustrate Foundation principles. For instance, the new Renton Community IKEA Performing Arts Center is another model of the private-public partnership in funding that was most appealing especially to Don Johnson. Impressed with the unique partnership of the Renton School District, the City of Renton, and the Renton Community Foundation, Kreielsheimer contributed $25,000 to its capital campaign. A new auditorium planned for the Renton High School was transformed into a community performing arts center partly named for IKEA, the private contributor who gave the most to its construction. In a ceremony resonant with heritage, the original brick cornerstone from the 1911 Renton High School was set on the foundation of the new center by three longtime Renton High School alumni.

When it opened in 1996 the Whidbey Island Center for the Arts (WICA) at Langley gave the second-largest island in the continental United States the presentation stage that it sorely needed. The Foundation directed a total of $135,000 to WICA, most of it as challenge grants for the center's capital campaign. Along with other contributors, the Foundation is thanked with a plaque in the theater lobby.

The extensive list of Kreielsheimer-supported regional venues also includes the Mount Baker Theatre, Bellingham's grand stage built in the 1920s. After its registration in 1978 as a National Historic Landmark, a wide consortium of private and public sources funded the restoration of the 1,509-seat "showplace of Whatcom County." For its part, the Foundation gave two $35,000 grants—the first in 1996 for a capital campaign titled "Act II—Raising the Curtain on the Future," and the second five years later, in 2000, as an unrestricted grant to the theater. During the same five-year period, the Broadway Center for the Performing Arts in Tacoma received six "special needs" grants and one matching grant designated for "management excellence" for a total of $26,704.

Naturally it was not uncommon for the requests arriving in the Foundation's mail to be somewhat grander than the Kreielsheimer check that was sent in return. For instance, the Capitol Theater in Yakima asked for $216,000 to replace its twenty-year-old sound system. Don Johnson awarded them $75,000, advising that the contribution "be presented as a kickoff or challenge grant to inspire other prospective donors to contribute the remaining two-thirds of the funds." While often these challenge grants required that the matching or remaining funds be accumulated before the stimulating grant would be awarded, in this case the check was enclosed with the encouraging suggestion.

The Village Theatre of Issaquah, the region's dedicated presenter of musical theater, was founded in 1979. In 1996 the Foundation gave $50,000 to the capital campaign to complete the Village Theatre in Issaquah, and four years later $100,000 more for another capital campaign. The Village Theatre first began to extend its mainstage season in 2000 when it also became the company-in-residence at the Everett Performing Arts Center. When all of its several programs and stages are figured together the company gives employment each year to over 500 artists.

Located in West Seattle, ArtsWest, a busy 149-seat theater and visual art gallery, is beloved region-wide for its imaginative and often delightfully good-humored presentations. Development Director Lori Dillon explains how the Foundation's challenge to this unique venue was a capper. "In the summer of 2000, ArtsWest received a $100,000 challenge grant for our capital campaign from the Kreielsheimer Foundation. The gift came at a crucial time in our campaign. The doors to our new facility had already opened, our first season was under way, and the capital campaign committee had just $250,000 (of $2,925,000) left to raise. By the end of August 2000, ArtsWest raised the necessary funds to meet the Kreielsheimer challenge and we successfully wrapped up the campaign. It is fascinating for me to look in our Kreielsheimer Foundation files and read articles about all of the incredible work that the Foundation did for the arts in our community. To know that ArtsWest is among the ranks of some of the largest and most established arts organizations in the city to have received funding from the Foundation is quite an honor."

In its support of the Harlequin Players of Olympia the Foundation helped save another historic motion picture theater that had gone dark — The State Theater in the state capitol's business core. The Harlequin's scrappy remodel of the old movie palace into an intimate stage for plays required less than two years. The effort resembled a mature version of the Mickey Rooney and Judy Garland film plots where kids valiantly mount their own shows largely on the strength of their youthful zest. Kreielsheimer helped them in 1999 with a $25,000 challenge grant for the renovation of The State. In his award letter to Scot Whitney, managing/artistic director of the Harlequin, Don Johnson explained, "a significant factor in the decision of the Foundation to make the grant has been the cooperative arrangement which you have entered into with Saint Martin's College to assist the Saint Martin's drama department's use of the State Theatre. We believe this is an example of very worthwhile cooperation between the college and Harlequin, ultimately providing significant benefits to the community." A second grant for $10,000 was sent to Harlequin in the spring of 2000. Tom O'Grady, Saint Martin's generous alum and benefactor had unexpectedly died, and Don Johnson asked that the gift honor his memory.

Charles Osborn gave Centrum at Fort Worden State Park in Port Townsend its first grant in 1987. It was a modest $2,500 for artists' residences. At that time, Osborn was also giving considerable aid to promising scholars of the Cornish College of the Arts. In 2000 Don Johnson presented the greatest part of Centrum's award, $25,000, as a "new classical music and dance grant." It was perhaps another example of the second co-trustee reiterating and so commemorating the work of the first co-trustee but with a greater sum. Centrum, created in 1973 by an alliance of the Washington State Arts Commission, the State Parks and Recreation Commission, and the Office of the Superintendent of Public Instruction, as a venue for almost every art activity — performances, workshops, festivals, residencies, and concerts — is an ideal example of a community arts center, except that in its case the community is the entire state.

Like Centrum and the Mount Baker Theatre, the Langston Hughes Performing Arts Center is at home in and thereby helps preserve a historic landmark, the Chevra Bikur Cholim congregation's temple in Seattle. Built in 1918 from plans drawn by Marcus B. Priteca, the Seattle architect known internationally for his designs of grand theaters like Seattle's Orpheum and the Paramount, the temple was purchased in 1972 by the Seattle Department of Parks and Recreation. The venerable sanctuary was then developed into the home for the arts center named after the author who was one of the great reflectors and creators of black culture in America. The Foundation gave $10,000 to the Langston Hughes Center for its All City Summer Musical in 2000, during the autumn of the Foundation's work.

Not far from Langston Hughes, the Rainier Valley Cultural Center also makes its home in a converted landmark, the historic Fifth Church of Christ Scientist. In the spring of 1998 the Foundation gave $15,000 to SEED — the Southeast Effective Development Inc. — for the first phase of renovations on the Columbia City landmark. The grant letter describes the goals expected of the new center as consisting of "programs focused on the arts, education, and multicultural activities and programs." Earlier, in 1982, Charles Osborn gave one of the Foundation's first grants to the Jewish Community Center (JCC). Following the standard of care given to black culture by the Langston Hughes Center, the JCC is concerned, by its own description, with "engaging the diverse population of Seattle's Jewish community for the purpose of education, recreation, and Jewish enrichment." At the time, Osborn's grant of $25,000 was a large one for the Foundation.

A decade before Don Johnson helped the Capitol Theatre with its lighting, another grant came to Yakima — one of the Foundation's earlier grants to a museum. With a plant of 65,000 square feet, the Yakima Valley Museum is big enough to have a Great Hall — the performing space where a variety of concerts are produced including *Drawing Room Diversions*, the popular series by the Yakima Valley Symphony. The Museum in Yakima's Franklin Park also has room to mount exhibits from its extensive collections on regional history, including a large assemblage of horse-drawn vehicles such as hacks, buggies, stagecoaches, and even a hearse. In 1989, Charles Osborn gave $25,000 that helped with an enlargement to the museum. Another early indication of Charles Osborn's taste for Western Americana was his support of the Western Washington Forest Industries Museum in Tacoma's Point Defiance Park. The Foundation gave three grants beginning in 1982 for capital improvements, campaigns, and programs, and a fourth and last grant in 1987 for the Museum's Camp Six restoration project. A total of $70,000 was contributed in support of this interpretive center for the history of the Northwest's most important extractive industry.

The Museum of Flight was another Kreielsheimer beneficiary with an interest in technology. Osborn gave $50,000 in 1985 toward the construction of the museum's expansive glass-curtain Grand Gallery, designed by Seattle architect Ibsen Nelson and completed in 1987. Don Johnson included the museum in the Foundation's grand finale of giving with a Foundation check for $100,000 marked for a film on the history of air transportation. *Time Flies—A Century of Flight* is played in a continuous loop on the several monitors in the thirty-four-seat 737 Airliner Theater built within the fuselage of the Boeing aircraft. At Don Johnson's request, the film has been identified by the Museum as a tribute to William M. Allen, the legendary Boeing president who guided the company into the age of passenger jets.

At the Museum of History and Industry (MOHAI), heritage and technology often go their own ways. However, with the Foundation's first grant of $25,000 to the institution, both interests were advanced together. Opening in 1997, the *Salmon Stakes* exhibit on the history of the North Coast salmon industry was a particularly appropriate subject for the Foundation to support, because the greatest source of the Kreielsheimer family's wealth was their salmon canneries in Alaska. This good match was not lost on trustee Johnson. His second and larger gift to MOHAI for $100,000 was a capital grant, no doubt for the institution's ongoing plans to move from its site in the Montlake Neighborhood to new downtown quarters in Seattle's expanded Convention Center.

The most favored Foundation grantee among all institutions that had anything to do with science and/or industry was the Pacific Science Center. Four payments of $250,000 each were directed to the Center over a two-year period from 1997 to 1999. They focused on assisting the Center in its capital campaign to expand and construct a new IMAX Theater on the southeast corner of its campus. In 2000, the Kreielsheimer Foundation added a $250,000 endowment challenge grant for the institution that has proven one of Century 21's (and Warren Magnuson's) best gifts to the city. The generous collective size of the gifts ($1,250,000) was another sign of the Foundation's traditional interest in institutions connected with the Seattle Center.

Both of the Kreielsheimer grants to the Woodland Park Zoo were extended to improve the habitats of its residents. The first was given by Charles Osborn in 1986, with $25,000 to the "Save Our Elephant Campaign," a project that greatly improved the Zoo's home for its pachy-

The new Jaguar Enclosure at Woodland Park Zoo

derms. (The elephant pledge was made in 1984 on condition that the campaign was a success.) In 2000, Don Johnson returned to Woodland Park and its Tropical Rain Forest with $1 million for the Zoo's Jaguar Enclosure that allows the big cats to roam through a much larger and more realistic environment than their former confines provided. As noted, both Greye Kreielsheimer and her daughter, Olivia, had a special affection for the Zoo and it was, in part, a response to that Kreielsheimer family attraction that led Johnson to make the sizable grant. It also helped that for twenty years Johnson had known and admired Dave Towne, the director of the Zoo. Johnson had acted as an attorney for the Washington Parks Commission, of which both Charles Osborn and Dave Towne were members.

The two largest Seattle museums with ethnic identities, the Nordic Heritage Museum in Ballard and the Wing Luke Asian Museum in the International District, received similar contributions from the Kreielsheimer Foundation: $114,140 and $108,000, respectively. Their use of the funds was also similar. In 1986 Charles Osborn gave the Nordic Heritage Museum $5,000 to help mount its *The Dream of America* exhibit. In 1995 Don Johnson sent $3,000 to the Wing Luke Asian Museum for its *Pioneer American Artist* exhibit. Osborn also helped Wing Luke with a $5,000 gift for installing equipment in its storage area. In the grand beneficence of the Foundation's last year Johnson gave $107,140 to the Nordic

Heritage Museum for its endowment and $100,000 to the Wing Luke Asian Museum for capital improvements. The latter museum's lengthy listing of the ways it used the capital is revealing of its many needs and services. The clipped prose of the in-museum report reads in part, "The $100,000 was used to create the Arts and Contemporary Issues gallery, rehab our front lobby, upgrade our classroom including a total rehab, new furniture and media center; underwrite upgrades of permanent exhibit; purchase public programs, furniture and equipment; support installation of technology upgrades."

The benefits given by the Foundation to three maritime beneficiaries are for projects that are for the most part sited together. At this writing, these are for the greater part projects that are still works-in-progress. Gifts of $50,000 to the Maritime Heritage Foundation, $150,000 to The Steamer Virginia V Foundation, and $1,000,000 to the City of Seattle all pertain to inclusion in the new South Lake Union Park of permanent moorage facilities for historic vessels, as well as a museum for other maritime interests and artifacts. The Foundation first joined this effort in the spring of 1996 when, along with several maritime groups, it gave its support to the second effort by the Seattle Commons proposal to persuade Seattle voters to permit development of the neighborhood south of Lake Union as a combination park and urban village. The Foundation's announcement of a $25,000 grant for feasibility studies toward the building of a maritime heritage center was timed for the vote.

While acceptance of the Commons campaign failed a second time, the maritime center project was still not abandoned although the interests — and vessels — of the several maritime groups were no longer tethered to the Commons. Instead, they proceeded to take the Foundation gift and create a plan for transforming a portion of the south shore into a maritime center. On July 1, 2000, Seattle Mayor Paul Schell received a deed to the more than five acres of the former naval reserve property, including the armory building at the south end of Lake Union. Don Johnson, who had previously advised his longtime friend the mayor that no Kreielsheimer grant was possible until the city had obtained title from the notoriously slow-acting federal government, was present to celebrate the event, and for the public announcement of the Foundation's expanded help. In an article that

Virginia V, ca. 1999

appeared the following month in *Shavings* (the publication for the membership of the Center for Wooden Boats, which — with Northwest Seaport,
United Indians of All Tribes, the Northwest Schooner Society, and The
Steamer Virginia V Foundation — constitutes the maritime consortium
pursuing the center), Mayor Schell called the Foundation's "surprising"
million-dollar gift "the largest any of us could remember in support of our
region's maritime heritage. . . . The Kreielsheimer gift will allow us to
rebuild the pier on the waterside of the armory for moorage of many of our
historic ships, the lightship *Relief,* the tug *Arthur Foss,* and the schooners
Zodiac and *Adventuress,* and the tall ship *Wawona.*"

   Although Don Johnson was also visualizing the *Virginia V,* the pier
that was built in part with the Foundation gift surprisingly used a system of
pilings neither sturdy nor flexible enough for the repeated transient moorage required by the 400 ton weight of the working *Virginia V.* Rather, the
proposed new pier was suited merely for the static moorage of secured vessels like the *Wawona.* The *Virginia V,* with its haunting steam whistle, was
built in an era when steamer docks were called landings, reflecting the reality that every docking was a variety of controlled crash. And in remaining
true to its type, the restoration of the historic steamer kept its old engine,

and thus its semi-maneuverable characteristics as well. Fortunately, at this writing, the city appears to have substantially completed fitting the pier with pilings that will allow for the repeated and adventurous landings of the *Virginia V.*

In 2000 the Kreielsheimer Foundation gave $150,000 toward restoration of the *Virginia V* just a few months after the Foundation had sprung its surprise gift of $1 million for the moorage. Earlier, in the mid-1990s, this last of Puget Sound's fabled Mosquito Fleet of steam-powered ships began its seven-year and $6.5 million restoration. The newly restored 122-foot passenger vessel was launched from the Lake Union Dry Dock at the southeast corner of Lake Union in the spring of 2002. As just noted, for Don Johnson the two grants were visualized together — the *Virginia V* protected alongside the pier subsidized by the Foundation.

11 | Alaska

After the last legal drinks were quaffed in public on December 31, 1915, and Prohibition became the law in Washington State, the by then more than quarter-century-old wholesale liquor business of the Kreielsheimer Brothers was necessarily abandoned. Thereafter, the accumulated wealth of the family and so also of its namesake Foundation was provided by the same creature that had sustained human culture along the North Coast for many millennia: the salmon.

Although not specifically noted in the will that created the Foundation, Alaska was easily enclosed within the general area named within it. Don Johnson explains, "Charlie interpreted the 'Pacific Northwest'—included within the will's geography of 'Puget Sound and the Pacific Northwest'—to encompass Alaska largely because Leo's canneries were in Alaska. Frankly, he had been given a heck of a lot of help from the natives, who froze their tails canning fish out in the Aleutians. I concurred that the least we could do was include them." Judging from the support given by the locals themselves, Alaska needed help. In the late 1990s, when most of the Kreielsheimer money that ultimately wound up in the far north was sent there; *The Chronicle of Philanthropy*, a print and online publication, ranked Alaskans earning more than $100,000 as forty-ninth in the nation for charitable giving.

In the effort to fund art in Alaska, the trustees were concerned—at least once to the point of consternation—about who was prepared to handle large grants in a state that is more than eight times the size of Washington but with a population density eighty times lower. Osborn and Johnson sent their greatest gifts north to two institutions, the Anchorage Museum of History and Art and the Alaska Native Heritage Center. The former is associated with Alaskan banker Elmer Rasmuson, a friend of both Osborn and Johnson, and founder of the Rasmuson Foundation, the state's most generous philanthropic agency. The latter was parented by the cultural activist Roy Huhndorf, who lightheartedly described himself to Johnson

Nathan Jackson carved this totem pole for the Alaska Native Heritage Centennial, Anchorage

as "one-half Native American and seven percent Jewish."

For four years, beginning with Osborn's gift early in 1992, the Anchorage Museum received $200,000 Kreielsheimer deposits into its endowment. Another $180,000 was directed toward exhibits and art acquisition, and a final $500 was given in memory of Elmer Rasmuson. Johnson alone gave to the Alaskan Native Heritage Center, also in Anchorage, the home for one-half of the roughly 600,000 Alaskans. His first two contributions from 1998 and 1999 for the institution's capital campaign were given gladly because of the trustee's admiration for Huhndorf, who performed the considerable diplomatic feat of convincing eleven of the state's thirteen tribes or nations to support the Center. In the end, $1 million of the Kreielsheimer gift to the Center was directed either to its capital campaign, as noted, or to its endowment. Another $75,000 paid for the monumental totem pole carved by Tlingit Master Carver Nathan Jackson. Near its center, Jackson's creation depicts a man who represents the Alaska Native Heritage Center opening the box of knowledge to be shared with the community. The pole was dedicated on August 23, 2003, near the entrance to the Heritage Center campus, and the ceremony was enacted in line with Tlingit protocol.

Another concern with Alaskan donations was distance. While Don Johnson did not think it was within the scope of the Foundation to send Seattle's Pacific Northwest Ballet to Scotland or Australia, he did consider

Alaska an appropriate alternative, but only if help was given. "We tried to work with the Alaska Dance Theatre and the Alaska Center for the Performing Arts in Anchorage and arrange for the Ballet to perform there. We agreed to give $100,000 to this project if Alaska Airlines could set aside a 737 to transport the dance company and/or the Seattle Symphony to the performance and back. If you take, say, eighty-eight people in an orchestra and put them in a halfway good hotel and then have to pay a roundtrip fare to Anchorage at regular rates it is a huge expense. In terms of cost for performance tickets you are back to hundreds of dollars a person. I was not about to squander the Kreielsheimer assets just because we could have done it." Instead, the Alaska Dance Theatre was given $50,000 by the Foundation but as a challenge grant for a new dance theater, not for helping host a costly visit north by Seattle dancers.[*] In the end, a troupe of dancers from PNB did visit Anchorage for a single performance sponsored by the Anchorage Concert Association in the spring of 1999. Although the cost was still a dear one, the $25,000 given by the Kreielsheimer Foundation to support the excursion was a quarter of the amount first considered.

The cost of miles traveled in the far-flung state — where one in every six residents is a pilot — was registered early on when Charles Osborn received from one of the tribes in the Alaskan Aleutian chain a request that would have tested both his gravity and credulity. The applicant asked for $100,000 toward a performance for an audience of 385 persons, in effect a subsidized ticket price of around $260 apiece. The first trustee declined, explaining that with the same amount the Foundation could benefit thousands in Seattle. The conservative Osborn did wind up guaranteeing a loan for a theater production in Anchorage that was more edgy than he had expected. The lobby floor was spread with an American flag, requiring patrons to walk on Old Glory to reach their assigned seats. In spite of this demonstration of not entirely free political speech (the patrons did have to pay for their tickets), the play and the desecration of the flag were not popular and the play soon folded, requiring the Foundation to make good the performing company's bad loan of $50,000 from the National Bank of Alaska. It was an isolated instance in which a Kreielsheimer disbursement wound up, so to speak, on the floor.

---

[*] See chapter 4 for more about Alaska Dance Theatre.

Elmer and Mary Louise
Rasmuson, ca. 1995

The Kodiak Baranof Productions of Kodiak received the earliest Foundation gifts to Alaska. The first was for programs in 1982, and three years later Charles Osborn called again with funds to help rehabilitate the Kodiak Auditorium. General support followed in 1986 for the related Kodiak Arts Council, and Osborn's last award was sent in the fiscal year 1987–88 for the renovation of *Cry of the Wild Ram*. Alaska's pageant of history and its longest running play is performed with a local cast, and has been called the "Oberammergau of Kodiak." Each of the four Kreielsheimer gifts was for $25,000 —a conventional Osborn sum. The first trustee also gave a total of $87,800 between 1985 and 1990 in support of the Visual Arts Center of Alaska. However, included in this amount was the $50,000 repaid to the National Bank of Alaska for the failed theatrical production noted above. In 1987 Osborn gave a small grant of $5,000 to the Pratt Museum for expansion and renovation. The Homer Society of Natural History operates the museum, and the variety of its exhibits and projects is exhilarating. Included are a historic homestead cabin, a forest ecology trail, a tide-pool tank, botanical gardens, and a sperm whale exhibition. The Pratt Museum also has a remote video link to Gull Island in Kachemak Bay, produces a variety of art exhibitions, and created the celebrated exhibit *Darkened Waters*, a profile of the *Exxon Valdez* oil spill of 1989. The list of grants sent by Osborn to Alaska is completed by the $25,000 he gave to Sheldon Jackson College in Sitka. Founded in 1878, it is the oldest educational institution to have been in continuous existence in the State of Alaska.

In addition to the two largest beneficiaries already noted—the Alaska Native Heritage Center and the Anchorage Museum of History and Art— Don Johnson gave to four more Alaska institutions. Perseverance Theatre is one of the principal cultural attractions in Juneau, the state capitol. Founded in 1979 it is known, among other things, for presenting more than fifty new plays by Alaskan and national playwrights, including Paula

Vogel's 1998 Pulitzer Prize–winning play *How I Learned to Drive*, which was also authored and developed at Perseverance Theatre. Kreielsheimer funding began there in 1997 with a $10,000 grant for the theater's In-Reach Program and concluded in 2000 with a sizable capital and endowment grant of $150,000.

Another stalwart of Alaskan culture, the Anchorage Concert Association, received a total of $75,000 from the Foundation, including the grant that sent Seattle's Pacific Northwest Ballet north to Alaska in 1999. Showing creativity, Johnson awarded the Koahnic Broadcast Corporation a general operations grant of $50,000 in the last year of the Foundation. This Alaska Native media center is repeatedly voted the best station in Anchorage. It features commercial-free music, news, and cultural, native, and local programming. Koahnic is Athabascan for "live air"; the station's call letters are KNBA 90.3 FM.

Completing this final quartet was a gift to Alaska Pacific University, which dedicated its campus in Anchorage on June 28, 1959, one day prior to statehood for Alaska. Late in its last year, 2000, the Kreielsheimer Foundation awarded this independent university a $100,000 grant for educational programs benefiting rural Alaska Natives.

On August 17, 1997, Don and Dottie Johnson joined a small group of trustees and directors of other charitable trusts on board the National Bank of Alaska's corporate jet for a tour of many of the state's cultural amenities. Johnson already knew Elmer Rasmuson, the group's host, but it was on this trip that he developed a deep admiration for the banker's personal qualities — the wisdom and wit that had in his lifetime influenced Alaskans of all sorts on the importance of preserving heritage and promoting art. Don Johnson's very last grant to Alaska was both his smallest and perhaps most heartfelt, given shortly after Rasmuson passed away. With the $500 sent to the Anchorage Museum of History and Art in memory of Elmer Rasmuson, the Kreielsheimer trustee noted, "I've always regarded him as the 'grand patriarch' of Alaskan philanthropy and certainly Alaska's 'number one citizen.' His gentle manner and quiet wisdom made a very deep impression on everyone."

12 | Northwest Art

The Kreielsheimer Foundation did not turn its eye aside from the popular albeit often nervous belief that a "Northwest Art" has been created out of Northwest influences. These insinuations are ordinarily described as some mix of nature and nurture, made from parts of spirit, weather, and position on the Pacific Rim. The tradition of a Northwest Art is also described as built from the influence of a "big four," artists who often listed themselves in this order: Mark Tobey, Morris Graves, Kenneth Callahan, and Guy Anderson. This shared impression has almost exclusively to do with visual arts, although there are those who recognize a provincial animus stirring in the literary arts as well. Readers of Northwest novelist Tom Robbins may, without knowing it, correctly intuit from his descriptions of the Northwest landscape that he was first an art critic. How many enclaves within the pantheon of Northwest Art have been fitted for named artists of all sorts depends upon who is doing the naming.

In her book *Iridescent Light: The Emergence of Northwest Art**, Deloris Tarzan Ament concentrates on twenty-one artists, and only a slim majority of Ament's candidates were still living at the time of its publication in 2002. While none of them are writers, a few like Tobey, William Cumming, and Wesley Wehr, could write quite well. The author includes two photographers, Johsel Namkung and Mary Randlett, among the twenty-one. Both are profound recorder-interpreters of the Northwest landscape, but Randlett, who has also collected the work of most of Ament's nominees — often in trade for her portraits of them — seems to channel a Northwest spirit. Consequently, both by the author's choice and necessity Mary Randlett, one of the subjects of the book, is also its principal photographer. The Kreielsheimer Foundation underwrote the production of *Iridescent Light*. To describe it too simply, Deloris Tarzan Ament's work is an enthusiast's search for a tradition that concludes by respecting its ambi-

* Ament, *Iridescent Light* (University of Washington Press and Museum of Northwest Art, 2002).

guities. Like most of us, Don Johnson knows what he likes about the art of the region. Unlike most of us he was in a position to generously support it. Following a lecture sponsored by the book's publishers, Ament told Don Johnson: "These artists — the ones I have written about — will deny that there is a Northwest School." Johnson answered, "Well I have had a similar problem while trying to make a grant to support it."

The last trustee, Johnson, managed to partially resolve this problem of Northwest identity by wisely relaxing its definition, in an alliance with the international tastes of Virginia and Bagley Wright. In the mid-1970s the Wrights, who were by then the region's greatest patrons and promoters of nonprovincial art, founded the Washington Art Consortium. The WAC was a circle of seven Washington State museums gathered together around the Wright's valuable collection of mostly New York–based art. When he wanted to pledge a million dollars to help promote Northwest Art it was suggested to Don Johnson that the Wrights' somewhat quiet Consortium might be enlivened by having its collection expanded to include contributions from Northwest artists past and present. Johnson's occasion for proposing this alliance came at an arts event that he and Virginia Wright were attending. After verbally sketching out his proposal of an alliance between the Foundation and the Consortium, as Johnson recalls, "Virginia pointed her finger at me and said 'call me.' " Johnson called, and the result was a cooperation that revitalized the Art Consortium with matching grants of $1,000,000 from Kreielsheimer and from Virginia and Bagley Wright. This promised infusion of funds required the Consortium to get organized, beginning with establishing its tax-deductible 501(c)3 status. Once given, the resources allowed Consortium members, the principal certified arts museums around the state, to inventory and coordinate their collections.

With the collections in order, the Consortium could also mount circulating exhibits of contemporary art from both the Northwest and elsewhere, much of which had been kept in passive retreat within the archives of one of the consortium members, Western Washington University. By compiling an inventory of art created in the Northwest and kept in both public and private collections it was reasonably expected that the participating institutions in WAC and others would be able — quoting here Sarah Clark-Langager, curatorial manager of the Consortium collection — "to make bigger and better exhibitions of Northwest Art." Borrowing a metaphor from a nonvisual art, Virginia Wright described this new harmony in a telephone message left for Johnson, "Don, I think we make beautiful music together."

Before crediting Kreielsheimer, Deloris Tarzan Ament writes in her introductory acknowledgements that her book *Iridescent Light* "was made possible by the Museum of Northwest Art, whose trustees supported its production." Of all the exhibitors in Washington State, the Museum of Northwest Art (MONA) in La Conner is most associated with the work of a Northwest School, both by name and practice. In line with Don Johnson's concern for supporting regional art, in 1995 the Foundation gave MONA two capital grants totaling $75,000 to help remodel the Wilbur Building, a nondescript commercial address on La Conner's First Street, into the tasteful new museum that opened on October 3, 1995, fourteen years to the day after the institution first began in one of La Conner's historic Victorian mansions.

The Museum of Northwest Art is also seen as helping to make up for what is thought by some to be the Seattle Art Museum's declining interest in regional art. It is an attitude that was perhaps heralded by SAM's now already ancient decision to drop the Northwest Annual in 1975. When Don Johnson revealed to Jack Benaroya that he intended to give to the La Conner museum, the philanthropist replied, "Well I might be interested in that." Earlier, Benaroya had granted $1 million to the Seattle Art Museum, expecting that the fourth floor Benaroya Gallery would be used as an exhibition space for regional art more than it actually was. The match to the Kreielsheimer grant that Jack Benaroya made to MONA created another Benaroya Gallery but this time in La Conner: a space within the new museum devoted to glass art. Jack and Rebecca Benaroya were also trustees of the Pilchuck Glass School that in 1995 celebrated its silver anniversary.

At the University Bookstore reception following her reading from *Iridescent Light*, Don Johnson asked author Ament, "Will emerging artists qualify? Is this 'Northwest Art' open or closed?" She responded, "Oh, definitely it's open."

In 1970 a new door was opened to a medium that would become globally associated with the Northwest — glass art. Charles Osborn gave the first grant from the Foundation to Pilchuck in 1985 — $50,000 for campus construction. Don Johnson returned to the glass art school in 1996 with a smallish grant of $5,000 for a hotshop at the school, but then added yearly amounts that lifted the total of Foundation gifts to Pilchuck to $422,860.

The second trustee's first gift to glass reached its home about eighty miles south of Pilchuck, going to the Tacoma Art Museum in 1994 — $10,000 toward the installation of Pilchuck veteran Dale Chihuly's installation at the city's restored Union Station. In all, $645,233 was given by the Foundation to the Tacoma Art Museum, $500,000 of it as a challenge grant for its building campaign in 2000. The lobby of the new museum features a permanent collection of early Chihuly glass in the Kreielsheimer Foundation Alcove. The Tacoma Art Museum also opened in the spring of 2003 with *Northwest Mythologies*, a survey of the Northwest School, with paintings borrowed from sources near and distant — like the Museum of Modern Art in New York. Feeling frisky in its new quarters, the Tacoma Art Museum claimed "no other museum survey anywhere has ever gone this far to show the interactions and mutual influence of the Big Four in the best possible light." The "Big Four," of course, are — in the alphabetical order the museum listed them — Guy Anderson, Kenneth Callahan, Morris Graves, and Mark Tobey. The Tacoma Art Museum followed its first show with *Building Tradition*, an exhibition it characterized as "highlighting the museum's unmatched commitment to the artists of our region."

Nearby the Tacoma Art Museum is another connection to glass art for both Tacoma and Kreielsheimer: the Museum of Glass. In 2000 the Foundation gave a $100,000 capital grant to the Museum of Glass toward the construction of its new quarters in the new Tacoma Cultural District.[†]

[†] Like the Tacoma Art Museum, five more Tacoma art institutions that received gifts from the Foundation feature the community name at the head of their own. From grants beginning in 1996 and continuing into 2001, the Tacoma Actors Guild received $26,503 from the Foundation and all of it was given through the Corporate Council for the Arts Special Needs Fund. The CCA also figures in seven Foundation outlays to the Tacoma Little Theatre, which received a total of $4,706 from Kreielsheimer. A similar sum, $5,000, was directed to the Tacoma Opera, and again all seven grants came through the services of the CCA. Holding to this convention of CCA mediation, the Tacoma Philharmonic, the Tacoma Symphony, and the Tacoma Youth Symphony all received similar Foundation gifts of $4,979, $5,066, and $5,286, respectively.

13 | Seeds, Niches, and Rescues

Throughout its active years the Foundation also proved its wit by responding to proposals that otherwise, according to Don Johnson, "would be lost in the niches of time." The Seattle Repertory Theatre's Shakespeare program that began in 2000 with a performance of *As You Like It* is a classic example of this niche-funding. As Christine O'Conner, then the Rep's director of development, put it. "There are not a lot of places we can go to get $1 million for four years of Shakespeare. There just aren't. That's a story best told to the Kreielsheimer Foundation."* The Foundation's avoidance of projects that "nobody else wants to do," as already noted, has often been suspended in the case of worthy proposals for which funding was otherwise hard to find. In its desire to have a work representative of late Renaissance Spanish painting added to its collection, the Seattle Art Museum responded "no" to Don Johnson's standard inquiry, "Do you have anybody else who is donating for this purchase?" When pressed, SAM explained candidly, "Well, very few in the community are currently interested in this kind of art but we still need it." Johnson agreed. "I had a little bit of concern but ultimately I believed that SAM should have representative works of art in other classic fields even if not in current vogue." Consequently the Foundation gave $25,000 to help with the Museum's acquisition of *The Virgin Presenting the Rosary to Saint Dominic* by the Spanish artist Antonio Palomino (1655–1726).

In 1988 Charles Osborn set a Foundation precedent for benefiting niche art when he joined Tom and Ann Barwick, Anne and John Hauberg, The Virginia Wright Fund, and the Nineteenth-Century Fund for museum purchases in procuring *Peonies Blown in the Wind*, by the nineteenth-century American artist John La Farge. The Foundation's part was fifty-eight percent of the $242,000 purchase price. At the time, the amount was a record paid for a stained glass window. In 1999 the Foundation also helped pur-

---

* And that story is also told by Jean Sherrard above in "Theatre" (chap. 3).

Portrait of George Washington by Rembrandt Peale, installed in the Governor's Mansion, Olympia, Washington

chase a painting of George Washington by Rembrandt Peale for the Governor's Mansion. This was a case of "a Washington for Washington" and so created another niche. Some unique projects supported by the Foundation brought with them pleasant surprises for the trustee. The late Janet Leigh, star of the 1960 Hitchcock thriller *Psycho*, appeared with the Northwest Chamber Orchestra for their playing of the music from the horror film.

The Kreielsheimer response to the plight of the Empty Space Theater in late 1992 may be read as a pure rescue story that has intimations of the cavalry (or Don Johnson as the Lone Ranger) coming over the hill. Johnson embarked upon his intercession after reading a letter to the editor in a local newspaper. He explains, "Someone wrote, in effect, 'For a lousy $90,000 are we going to let this great theater die?' " Jean Sherrard tells this story above in his essay in chapter 3 on Foundation contributions to local theater.[†]

Perhaps the earliest Foundation rescue was Charles Osborn's response

[†] Sherrard also charts the Foundation's 1995 answer to the Group Theater's emergency campaign to eliminate its operating debt in order to qualify for a second round of support from the National Arts Stabilization Fund. The annual tasks of paying rent, insurance, staff, publicity, stagecraft, and actors can never be met by ticket prices alone. Of the many midsized theaters that received Kreielsheimer funding the Group Theater was one of only three that have subsequently gone dark. The others are the Bathhouse Theater and the Alice B. Theater. And while the Empty Space has survived, it has had, like many other performing groups, to reduce staff and programming to navigate the more recent tough times.

to Mayor Charles Royer's panel on the fiscal predicament of the Seattle Symphony in the summer of 1986. Eleven days after reporting on the panel's recommendation that the troubled orchestra be given rent-free use of the Opera House, the local dailies could trumpet that Kreielsheimer had granted the Symphony $300,000 to help them in their emergency. At the time it was the third-largest grant given in Seattle Symphony history, a statistic that puts the Orchestra's successful funding campaign a decade later in remarkable perspective. (As noted earlier, the combined Benaroya Hall/SSO endowment drives reaped more than $150 million.) Later in 1986, the City Council—on a seven-to-one vote—made its own appropriation of $220,000 to the Orchestra. While its problems were then considerably more grave than any half million could fix, Symphony President Jim Gillick noted that the city's response was still "important as a leadership gift." And so too was the Foundation's.

14 | Art at the Edge

It was probably his sense of humor that rescued Don Johnson from the nervous concerns that can too often unsettle anyone selected to make and balance decisions of taste and need while funding the serious and sometimes esoteric arts. Surveying the popular culture about him Johnson has concluded, "Frankly, I am over the hill. I don't know who most of these current movie and television stars are." While Leo and Greye Kreielsheimer did not exclude any of the arts from their philanthropy, they were certainly most interested in the established ones like the opera and the art museum, and considered gifts given to them as most likely to be lasting contributions. The Foundation's two individual trustees were both sensitive to Leo and Greye's settled tastes. The second trustee — like Leo in his yellow Corvette — was also sometimes ready to take a risk. Don Johnson understood that because the arts are creative there is in them a strong urge to experiment. His shorthand for art that is so preoccupied is "edge art."

Most artists do not get much popular attention, even the more accomplished among them. In a society with fundamental rights of self-expression, controversy and artful outrage can be mixed forms of expression, protest, and even marketing. Still, by pop-star standards the names of the avant-garde are nearly hermetic — excepting those who may either by design or accident trigger some taboo involving religion, family, sex, or nation. For these artists, receiving the help of patrons and philanthropists is an especially rare event. More often this risky art has been supported with public funds. In 1973, at the time Leo Kreielsheimer was first meeting with his lawyer Charles Osborn to create a posthumous foundation in support of Northwest Art, the Seattle Arts Commission was increasingly inclined to nurture programs that emphasized public art. The work of the emerging artists that made it was often quite edgy. Both of the multiday arts festivals at Seattle Center — Bumbershoot and Folklife — were then in their populist infancies. The One Percent for Art Program and later the Hotel–Motel tax fraction for the arts continued this by now Seattle-wide emphasis on the relevance of community-engaged art and support of the artists who create it.

The experimental side of theater can test one's sensibility both on stage and off; it requires of patrons and donors a progressive attitude at best — or at a minimum at least a philosophical distance. Given the many new stages made possible with aid from the Kreielsheimer millions, it is inevitable that the Foundation has indirectly supported the performance and/or display of a large sampling of art that would not be described as either popular or fine but rather as experimental — and sometimes too experimental for someone or something. Don Johnson reflects, "One knows pretty much that the Seattle Symphony and the Seattle Opera will do a great job. However, in theater there is probably more variation in a season's programming. I have been to more plays where the production is just the greatest thing I have seen in years and the next one seems to use the theater as simply a vehicle to send a bunch of thinly veiled political messages. That is just the way it works." And yet by Don Johnson's judgment, one of the favorite plays he saw as trustee was a performance by the Book-It Repertory Theatre of Peter Parnell's stage adaptation of the John Irving novel *Cider House Rules*, a contemporary play with considerable daring.

Since its 1997 "baptism" with the *Cider House Rules*, the Rep's intimate Leo Kreielsheimer Theatre (aka the Leo K. Theatre) has also staged its share of low comedy, satire, political rant, and experimental dance. *Alpha Tango* by Gita Govinda is a good example. It was one of nineteen dance pieces performed by a variety of emerging artists on the Leo K. stage during the 1997 ArtsEdge festival sponsored by Paul Allen's Experience Music Project. As a precaution for its potential audience each dance was rated for nudity, violence, and sexual content. The *Alpha Tango* program described the dance as "The epic Indian love poem of Krishna and Radha, featuring original multi-ethnic music, narration, and color slides — and nudity." It was rated "adult."

The most consistent nurturer of art-at-the-edge in Pugetopolis has been On the Boards[*], and about On the Boards Don Johnson is at once sensitive and practical. "They have lasted, they are good people, and they are trying. By my somewhat old-fashioned standards they get over the edge sometimes and have probably done some things that I wouldn't care for,

---

[*] Ultimately the Foundation gave $833,490 to On the Boards, a story told in greater detail by Genevieve McCoy in chapter 4.

but that's okay. I liked the concept of bringing the avant-garde into town and having a fine place to present it, so we helped them with their capital campaign."

There are also a few examples of the Kreielsheimer Foundation giving direct support to uncommon — if not experimental — programs. After the Seattle Symphony chose a downtown site for its new hall rather than the K block, the Foundation adjusted part of its funding for the orchestra toward support for programming. Don Johnson recalls, "Seattle Symphony conductor Jerry Schwarz told me that he'd like to do some concert operas where the music is done without costume changes and acting. Schwarz was concerned that many classics of American stage music were not being heard for want of the wherewithal to produce them. I thought that was a very legitimate proposal and I granted them $100,000 for it, money that their regular programming budget really could not justify." The gift helped produce two concert opera performances of music from Howard Hanson's opera *Merry Mount* in 1996, when the Orchestra was still playing in the old Opera House. Three hundred and twenty-five performers were involved in the production of *Merry Mount,* including adult and children's choruses, with an expanded orchestra, besides the principal singers. The concerts were also another medal for Schwarz the conductor to pin on the lapel of Schwarz the Hanson revivalist and the Orchestra's successful campaign to bring back the Howard Hanson oeuvre. Other Kreielsheimer grants to the Seattle Symphony helped with concert versions of the opera *Peter Ibbetson* by composer Deems Taylor and Igor Stravinsky's opera-oratorio *Oedipus Rex.* A quarter-million dollars of the Foundation's last large disbursement to the Orchestra was directed toward special programs as well, including Janáček's *Glagolitic Mass,* performed in the 2000–2001 season.

Part IV

Legacy:
The Kreielsheimers
and the Trustees

Part IV concentrates on subjects — the Foundation's founders, their forebears, and their charges, the trustees — all of which, while present throughout the book, often remain in the wings. Here they are given center stage. In this respect, the philosophical and social sources for the founder's philanthropy are also considered, and a few of the personal touchstones connected to the trustee's choices are explored.

The Kreielsheimer Foundation: Creation, Structure, and Philosophy

In 1975, the year it was created, the Kreielsheimer Foundation bucked the populist currency then being traded in the arts. That year the national Associated Council of the Arts (ACA) for the first time in its then ten-year life gave undivided attention to what the prospectus to its annual conference described as "the solitary artist—the painter, sculptor, playwright, poet, writer, composer, choreographer—rather than the performer." That year the Seattle Arts Commission, an ACA member, increased its direct services to individual artists through an enlarged Art In Public Places program. It also continued to employ "solitary artists" to do their art through its Artist-in-Residence program, largely funded by Richard Nixon's federal employment program, CETA: the Comprehensive Employment and Training Act.

If Leo Kreielsheimer knew about these trends he was most likely not concerned with them. Instead he created a charitable foundation whose primary support to the arts would go to those established stalwarts—the opera, the symphony, dance, and so on—where excellence in performing are most clearly established. The Foundation of course also supported individual artists, but almost always indirectly through the institutions or organizations that sponsored their shows or performances. When the Foundation gave $37,000 to the Skagit Valley artist Richard Gilkey in 1984 after he crushed several vertebrae in a collision with a semi truck it was not an outright grant but for purchase of three paintings. The tethering of the Gilkey grant to arts institutions then followed the form set by Charles Osborn, the first trustee, who made gifts of the three paintings— one each—to Cornish, the Seattle Art Museum, and the Henry Art Gallery. Gilkey used a few thousand of the largess to finish his studio. Inadvertently, it was perhaps the smallest capital grant given by a foundation that would later disperse much of its wealth toward helping put new roofs over the heads of many of the region's arts institutions.

Confident that Charles Osborn, his energetic lead lawyer, would see out the millennium, Leo Kreielsheimer protected his vision for the Foundation by prescribing that it complete its giving by the year 2000. And if Charles Osborn should prove less robust than expected, Leo named Don Johnson, another Bogle & Gates lawyer whom he liked and with whom he worked, to take over. The rare role of the individual trustee is stated in the Kreielsheimer will, as described by Don Johnson in his preface. In the event of a disagreement over allotments between the individual trustee in charge of the giving and the corporate trustee entrusted with investing, it was the former who would have precedence. Osborn would never need worry about ending up debating over grant awards with an employee of the bank trustee who perhaps might have insufficient understanding and/or sympathy for Leo and Greye's intentions. This special emphasis on the guardian power of a trusted personality was a kind of laying on of hands, and Charles Osborn and Don Johnson were the anointed ones.

Don Johnson explains it this way: "The concern with a bank or corporation acting as principal trustee is that with such a large group at some point the question will likely surface — 'Who in that organization is making the decisions?' With the Kreielsheimer Foundation such a question would not arise. The bank would hold the assets and invest them, and the gift-making decisions would be vested in the individual trustee. These two would have quarterly meetings — more if needed — to review the investments and make recommendations for changes. In this the bank trustee would also have a vote, but it would not be a controlling vote." In his legal practice focused on tax and estate planning, Charles Osborn chose to allocate more of his available time to investment management than did Johnson. When Johnson took over in 1992 he faced the fortunate and ironically demanding results of Osborn's restraint. Given the general momentum of the investment markets at that time, the Foundation's assets continued to grow — and surprisingly so. "I had neither the time nor the ego to think that I was any better at investing than others who were more experienced in it than I. During my time it was the bank, the investment firm of Badgley, Phelps and Bell and myself who made up the investment committee. I generally went along with their recommendations. I had some doubts about some of our real-estate decisions, but given the overall investment successes, to object would have been quibbling. My challenge was to figure out how best to give away $50 million and, with less than a decade remaining, to accelerate the rate of giving."

In choosing how to fulfill Leo and Greye's wishes, the Kreielsheimer trustees had to select from four classes of requests. If listed psychologically, that is, by how immediate and sometimes alarming the need was, the proposals ran from anxious cries for help with operating budgets, to requests for "sponsorship" of specific productions, to polished campaigns for grander purposes like building new facilities, and finally to prudent efforts to fill endowments for insuring the future. Increasingly, it became the Kreielsheimer philosophy that it is for want of the fourth item, endowments, that many arts organizations are chronically worried about the first one, paying for the next day or even yesterday. Consequently, the uniquely powerful position of both the individual trustees—Charles Osborn and Don Johnson—to make choices of how much to give and to whom, was tuned to funding capital campaigns and endowments. Often the Foundation's answer for an applicant's worrisome detailing of their daily difficulties was a mildly ironic focusing on—and often funding of—long-range plans, and not instant relief. In this there was also considerable leverage, especially on the part of Don Johnson, who dispersed nearly eighty-six percent of the total $100 million plus Kreielsheimer largess.

From the descriptions of many who worked with him, Johnson was very good at recognizing and working strategically with what he termed the critical mass that was required for building distinguished structures and/or establishing security. The example—and prestige—of an early Kreielsheimer grant was often enough to stimulate or outright challenge the philanthropic community and motivated city and county councils to make similar and matching gifts so that the "really big things" could happen. As revealed many times in the foregoing chapters and as further elaborated below, the two trustees also planted many seeds, filled neglected niches, and managed to make a few heroic rescues. After Don Johnson put on the mantle of individual trustee following Charles Osborn's death in 1992, he decided to discard the last three of the six categories of applicants as expressed in a Guidelines document prepared in the 1980s by Osborn. These were: (4) general education, (5) medical research and facilities, and (6) social services.

That left (1) visual and performing arts, (2) art education, and (3) public facilities, such as park or recreational facilities that would include artistic and/or educational elements. Johnson explains that the dismissed categories were "far afield from arts and education and, as a practical matter, were not being funded. It was misleading. By including them in the Guidelines we were giving false encouragement." Suggestions that the Foundation might also have stated outright a preference for funding art institutions over individual artists would, because of the significant exceptions, have been a sacrifice of alternatives for the Foundation, even if rare ones. Leo and Greye Kreielsheimer of course could not have wanted their trustees to play for them a posthumous guessing game about which requests to fulfill. Therefore Leo Kreielsheimer's will states clearly that the fortune be directed toward the arts and education. Greye Kreielsheimer, who lived five years beyond her husband's passing, by her own choice also distributed the majority of her wealth to the Foundation upon her death in 1980.

Given the plethora of deserving grantees, it is easier to describe the protocol of the trustee's choices in the negative; that is, what they perceived Leo and Greye did not want. The couple was direct in prescribing that their gifts should not to go religious organizations except in situations where those organizations used the gifts intrinsically for the arts. Charles Osborn's early grants to both Seattle and Gonzaga universities, both Roman Catholic institutions, were given for arts projects. The Tsutakawa fountain installed at Seattle University with Foundation funding initiated by Osborn was, by his successor Don Johnson's reckoning, "a classic example of giving incredible art. The community was the beneficiary. Now if the Kreielsheimer gift were directed to the Bishop's Fund or something similar that would have been another thing." One of Johnson's own heartfelt distributions was made to another small Catholic college, Saint Martin's, near Olympia. Again it was for their new arts building, named the Kreielsheimer Hall Arts Center. Similarly, there are many examples of Foundation distributions going to youth-oriented organizations but nearly always for arts related projects.

One of the principal talents required of a trustee is the knack of being able to voice a gracious "no." As Don Johnson recalled, "Charlie's excuse for not funding a proposal was that the Foundation was 'fully committed.' He would explain, 'Although you have a very worthwhile project we are not in a position to give.' " The status of a Foundation trustee resembled that of a rich uncle without direct heirs but with plenty of talented nephews, nieces, and cousins. Don Johnson resisted the temptations. "It was clear, of course, that practically everyone who came into the office, whether they stated it or not, wanted money. But the work of the Foundation was not about what would make Charles Osborn or Don Johnson liked and admired. The issue for the trustee was whether that money was going to be expended properly to accomplish the purposes that Leo Kreielsheimer wanted. You can ask any trustee—and this goes with the territory of managing foundations of philanthropic gifts of deceased persons—no one can be certain that what is done is exactly what they would have wanted done. And yet I am very satisfied that we did not do anything of significance which Leo would not have approved."

Since there are always many more requests received than gifts given, the psychology of asking is ordinarily tinged with at least some foreboding. For institutions on the edge, every request that is floated to a foundation rides on a tide of anxiety. Waiting for the answer can be rather like expecting a medical report. Understandably, applicants who are not funded are the most critical of any foundation that fails them. Sometimes even "winners" may feel slighted, for as a general rule less is given than is asked for. Don Johnson recalls granting $85,000 to one group that asked for $3 million. When asked how they could imagine that they would receive a grant of the magnitude they requested they answered, "Well, there's no harm in asking."

In actuality criticisms of the Foundation were rare. Throughout his recollections the last trustee shows considerable affection for many who made requests of Leo and Greye's philanthropy, even for those who did not ultimately receive it. Johnson discovered sympathetic and sometimes heroic qualities in many of the advocates who came for support. Obviously, a person chosen by an art organization to promote its development must be committed and confident in that assignment. Some may even seem entitled through sheer bravura. Johnson notes, "They are also all underpaid."

Don Johnson was earnest in explaining—when it was necessary—that "the Kreielsheimer Foundation is not about spreading the Kreielsheimer name all over town. It is about fulfilling the intentions of Leo and Greye Kreielsheimer." There was, however, no hiding the Kreielsheimer light behind a stage curtain. Often the Foundation's contributions to capital campaigns were of such a size that a "rule of admiration" required that the name be put in the spotlight and held there. In his essay above on Foundation gifts to theaters, Jean Sherrard tells the charmed story of how the "Leo K." theatre got its name when the Rep attached it to the Bagley Wright Theatre. In agreeing to the abbreviated "Leo K." name, Don Johnson may have called forth memories of the puckish Leo whisking about town in his yellow Corvette. Curiously, the abbreviation has often been disregarded. For instance, the Leo K. Theatre continues to be, in almost every instance of its appearance on the Internet, referred to in whole as the Leo Kreielsheimer Theatre. From all its applications the name "Kreielsheimer" is used more in reference to this little "jewel box" theater than any other. And there are plenty of others.

An incomplete inventory of where and how the Kreielsheimer name has been applied — and not merely on lobby plaques but to places like halls, centers, and promenades, and to programs and "chairs" — includes, beside the Repertory Theatre's Leo K. Theatre, ACT's Kreielsheimer Place, the Kreielsheimer Gallery in the Bellevue Art Museum, the Kreielsheimer Hall Art Center at Saint Martin's College, the Intiman Theatre's Greye Kreielsheimer Rehearsal Space, the Kreielsheimer Promenade at the courtyard to the Marion Oliver McCaw Hall at Seattle Center, the position of the Leo Kreielsheimer Professor of Fine Arts at Gonzaga University in Spokane, and the Kreielsheimer-endowed Scholarship Program at Cornish College of the Arts. And there is also a list of what may be called "lost names." Someday a card game of Seattle arts trivia may ask the question, "What were the first proposed names for both the Benaroya Hall and the McCaw Hall?" Flip the card over and the players will read "Kreielsheimer." The admirable fact is that the Kreielsheimer Foundation was ready to give up naming rights in order to help insure that big capital projects were fulfilled.

The story of the Kreielsheimer legacy is a substantial testimony to the power of wealth when it is given away. That Leo Kreielsheimer made it onto the community's Sesquicentennial list of the 150 most influential citizens in Seattle's first 150 years is like an official thank-you card sent posthumously to the philanthropic couple. It would be fair to describe the

Foundation's sole two individual trustees, Charles Osborn from 1975 to the summer of 1992, and Don Johnson for the duration, as the charmed producers for Leo Kreielsheimer's successful sesquicentennial candidacy. Clearly, Leo's visionary decision to cross the line from merely multiplying the wealth made by his forebears and himself through liquor, leather, and fish to transforming it into the expressive and unique effects gained from giving grants for the arts and education has made its historic impact. Years hence the buildings and halls and plaques that carry the Kreielsheimer name will be razed and replaced one by one. But the Kreielsheimer legacy will continue to make its mark, because the arts are instructive and the lessons they bring are passed along through the generations by the recurring cycle of students becoming teachers — and audiences.

16 | Pioneers and Patronage

Patrons of the arts on a grand scale posthumously, Leo and Greye Kreielsheimer were also regular supporters while they were living, although hardly showy ones. As Sheila Farr notes in chapter 2, the couple's own collection of paintings revealed an appreciation for artists in the extended Northwest School. Their daughter, Olivia, remembered that the opera was on the radio much of the day every Saturday. They also frequented live performances by the local symphony and opera and were active supporters of both as well as of the Seattle Art Museum. But the couple was not as involved in the inner sanctums of Seattle's art society as were some of their contemporaries, for example Hans and Thelma Lehmann. In 1992 the Lehmanns published a revealing reminiscence of their zestful swim in the Seattle fine-arts scene that followed the doctor and his artist wife's move here in 1936. The title of their book *Out of the Cultural Dustbin* (Crowley Associates, 1992) alludes to one of the more humbling moments in the history of local art propriety.

In 1942, his second year as conductor of the Seattle Symphony, Sir Thomas Beecham described Seattle culture as a "dustbin." (It might have been better compared to a mudroom.) Leo would surely have known of Beecham's sweeping criticism soon after it spread through the dailies, but did he also earlier attend the English maestro's first concert with the Seattle Symphony — sitting perhaps behind the Lehmanns who were in the first row? On the verge of the downbeat for *A Walk in a Paradise Garden*, by Delius, Beecham heard a click from the camera of the *Post-Intelligencer* photographer Art French, sitting in his reserved seat near the stage and the Lehmanns. Swiftly turning and pointing his baton at the newsman the conductor ordered him to "get out." (Another account has it, "Leave this hall. This is an insult to the audience.") It was Seattle's commanding introduction to both Delius's *Paradise* and the somewhat fussy English peer who thereafter could not direct a good review out of the morning paper.

Leo Kreielsheimer and Sir Thomas Beecham both resided at the same prestigious First Hill address, the Marlboro House, but at different times. By

1942 Leo and his mother, Olivia, were already three years out of the Marlboro and into their Denny Blaine neighborhood mansion beside Lake Washington. When the home was purchased from Elsie Dunbar in 1939 (the deed was flown by the China Clipper from Hong Kong where Dunbar lived), it was the largest residential sale in the city that year. The finest feature of the real estate was its terraced gardens that stepped between the home and the lake through a lot 350 feet deep. The mansion in which Leo and Greye raised their family remains one of the finest of domestic settings in a city that is celebrated for them. Still, at the time of Beecham's unpleasant remarks Seattle was beginning to fancy itself as having built a variety of class that reached beyond the merely picturesque sort, such as being surrounded by a charmed landscape or a location having a big footprint of waterfront garden property in Denny Blaine. Of course, the message behind the Lehmann reminiscence is that a half-century after Beecham had returned to the well-swept salons of England Seattle had done a lot of dusting.

Curious (and often extraordinarily snobby) European tourism of the West began in earnest in May 1869, when the first transcontinental railroad was completed upon the joining in Utah of the Union Pacific Railroad coming from the east and the Central Pacific Railroad coming from California made it suddenly possible to come this way quickly and, by the previous standards of saddles and even buckboards, relatively smoothly. Maestro Beecham also came west by rail — no doubt in a Pullman — and his knock on Seattle was a latter-day variation of an Old World theme. Perhaps the most trumpeted study had come sixty years earlier thanks to the wit of Oscar Wilde during his 1883 visit. Wilde found signs of art west of the Rockies "infinitesimal." For his English readers he wrote famously of "an art patron — one who in his day had been a miner — [who] actually sued the railroad company for damages because the plaster cast of Venus de Milo, which he had imported from Paris, had been delivered minus the arms. And, what is more surprising still, he gained his case and the damages."

In 1836, through a four-and-a-half month season (when Seattle founder Arthur Denny was still a fourteen-year-old helping his parents on their Illinois farm), the English soprano Anna Bishop appeared in over forty major London concerts at Vauxhall Gardens, Drury Lane, and the homes of aristocracy, often with the most famous European performers of the day, including a young Felix Mendelssohn. In his 1924 book, *Seattle and Environs, 1852–1924,* magistrate and pioneer chronicler Cornelius Hanford judges Bishop's 1873 appearance here as the first visit to Seattle of a famous singer. When still a young virtuoso with great technique (although by one assessment limited power in the low register) Bishop launched a nearly lifelong career of making the worldwide concert tours, one that eventually brought her from the railhead on San Francisco Bay by ship to concerts in Victoria, Seattle, and Olympia. Those who heard her, despite the acoustics compressed by the low ceiling of Yesler's Pavilion, understood that through this distinguished representative they were in touch with London high culture. In her prime Bishop was considered indisputably at the top of English opera performers, although even that stature remained, in the attitude and altitude of London society, one rung below Italian talent.

As Hanford describes it, during her Seattle visit Dame Bishop was invited to the home of Mrs. Linna W. J. Bell, "the center of musical activity at that time" and entertained by Seattle's best musical talents, the Bell daughters Lizzie and Lillian. Of course, the prestige of playing host to an international star is a perennial itch for local patrons and players.

The sweet singing of the Bell sisters and others like them in local living rooms, churches, and schools was the seed for what would through Seattle's boom years, beginning in the 1880s, become a landscape of homemade culture with singing societies, living-room operettas, and a strong musical curriculum at the University of Washington. All were performing, of course, almost exclusively from European scores. In the relatively unmediated years before the entertaining distractions of radio and television, these amateur talents were the greatest part of the musical culture in Seattle. The part played by the renowned talents that visited Seattle — such as the violinist Camilla Urso in 1875, who carried the first Stradivarius across the gangplank to Yesler's wharf — was just the frosting.

In 1881 Seattle surpassed Walla Walla as the largest town in Washington Territory. When the Northern Pacific Railroad completed its line in 1883 to New Tacoma, a town created and marketed by the railroad at the side of "old" Tacoma, it was the older port alongside Elliott Bay, with its greater range of opportunities — rather than the railroad's own stolid company town on Commencement Bay — that ultimately benefited the most from the mass migration that came with the transcontinental rail link. The young lawyer and future judge Everett Smith came fresh from Yale Law School to scout the city in 1885. He found a town that he assured his reluctant fiancée Mary by letter was "Cosmopolitan? I should say so. Walk down Front Street [First Avenue] any day and you meet Chinese, Indians, Irish, Negroes, Italians, Germans, Jews, French, English, and Americans from every state. I never saw such a great small metropolis."

Seattle got its first opera house, the Squire, in 1879 and its second, the Frye, in 1884. When new, with its mansard roof and center tower, the Frye was described as the best stage north of San Francisco. In their time both were busy with performances by local and visiting talents. For instance the St. John's Musical Society of Olympia mounted Gilbert and Sullivan's *Mikado* — then all the rage — at the Frye. The *Post-Intelligencer* review proffered another London allusion when it was especially impressed with "Mr. Woodruff as Poo Bah . . . His impersonation of the 'Lord High Everything Else' was capitally done. We have seen the same part played at the Savoy in London and are bound to say that Mr. Woodruff's work will bear comparison."

17 | The Kreielsheimer Brothers

The *Mikado* was performed in the spring of 1887, the year that Jake and Simon Kreielsheimer arrived in Seattle from Germany by way of El Paso. They found a community that was cosmopolitan in the extreme and working on its sophistication. Their youngest brother, Max, soon followed them, and their timing was perfect. Seattle was at the first curve in its time trial of qualifying as a great American boomtown. In the thirty years between the censuses of 1880 and 1920, Seattle galloped from a population of about 3,500 to more than 230,000. Following the city's Great Fire of 1889, the three brothers built their own business block on the city's busiest arterial, Commercial Street (now First Avenue South). By then, as the Kreielsheimer Bros., they were already prospering, with their double niche in wholesale liquor and leather. Later, when Prohibition drove the spirits underground, they kept the leather but substituted salmon for liquor.

The brothers prospered in part because they made a pact to prosper, along with a Spartan plan that allowed for little else, postponing romance, marriage, and other delicacies. Leo and Greye's daughter, Olivia T., was especially fond of this Kreielsheimer family story because it was her grandfather Max, the youngest brother, who broke the pact and married her grandmother and namesake Olivia A. Thornton on the sly. At first Leo was raised in the home of his in-laws the Thorntons. He was, apparently, well beyond diapers when his existence was revealed to uncles Jake and Simon. Jake died not long after, in 1915, when Leo was five years old, and Simon followed in 1926. Leo's father lived nine years more. That Max was probably the least ascetic — or most connected — of the brothers is revealed in his obituary, where he is listed as a charter member of both the Arctic Club and the Nile Temple of the Shrine and a member as well in both the B'nai Brith and Temple de Hirsch congregations.

With his mother Olivia, Leo was the executor of his father's will. It included one prohibition that was a reflection of the grim times. It reads, "Because of the conditions existing in Germany, under which my benefici-

Kreielsheimer Bros. advertisements, ca. 1890s

aries there residing would not be fully able to control and/or remove their property or money therefrom, I direct that my executors do not pay the bequest to any of my devises who may be residing in Germany at the time of my death while they continue to reside there." Max died on November 12, one week after he signed his will. It was nearly three years since Hitler had been named German chancellor, and three years before Kristallnacht (November 9–10, 1938), when more than a thousand synagogues were burned, and about seven thousand Jewish businesses vandalized and looted in Germany, and he must have sensed worse was to come.

Max left the bulk of his estate — the dailies put it between $500,000 and $1,000,000 — to Olivia and Leo. The short list of his callings included president of the Kadiak Fisheries Company, secretary-treasurer of the Northwest Leather Company, a director of the Seattle Brewing and Malting Company, and owner of both the Hungerford and Arcadia hotel properties. With the death of his father, Leo, a 1932 graduate from the UW School of

Max and Olivia Thornton Kreielsheimer,
ca. 1905

Business, suddenly stepped from assisting his father with the family businesses to running them. It was a role that he played with considerable success, evidenced first by the advance of the family's fortunes and ultimately by the contributions of his namesake foundation. Leo's daughter, Olivia, recalled how each morning on his way to work her father performed a whimsical ritual of appreciation to her grandparents, Max Kreielsheimer and Olivia Thornton Kreielsheimer. Toward their portraits, mounted side-by-side on the face of an armoire in the hall of the family home, the puckish Leo would pivot, click his heels, and bow an offering thanks, and then ask his forebears to wish him luck before turning again for the front door.

Leo married Greye McCormick as World War II was approaching, and together, in the elegant and comfortable setting of the Denny Blaine home, they reared two sons, Simon and Max (named for a granduncle and grandparent), and Olivia (named for her grandmother). Tragically, both boys died before their parents. Leo was sixty-five when he died in 1975, and although he did not

Leo and Greye Kreielsheimer, early 1940s

reach a ripe old age, like his father, Max, he had lived a life that was engaged. Leo was a member of both the Harbor Club and the Washington Athletic Club. His leadership qualities are indicated by his positions as a director for the King Crab Institute as well as officer and trustee of the Association of Pacific Fisheries. The Salmon canneries at both Kadiak and Chignik were his principal Alaskan concerns and sources of his fortune. In and near Seattle he continued the work of investments and property management, begun by his father and uncles as the Kreielsheimer Bros. firm. Only Olivia survived to witness the active life of the Kreielsheimer Foundation, including its charmed crescendo of success in the 1990s. Olivia's principal influence on the Foundation's choices was in favor of the Woodland Park Zoo, a city institution that was also loved by her mother. The Zoo was one of the exceptions to the Foundation's primary interest in the region's performing arts. In the summer of 2002 Olivia died suddenly, leaving two daughters, Ammine and Courtenay Berry.

As part of the second wave of pioneers, the Kreielsheimer brothers were not required to be as hardy as the trailblazers, just better heeled. The brothers cannily carried their nest egg to what in 1887 was obviously a boomtown going places fast. By the late 1880s the pioneer importance of sweat labor had long been surpassed by the work of wealth and law, though they were often combined. As often as not in this second migration it was the profession of law that was the most influential. Attorneys brought suits and bought real estate. They read torts and ran for office. They wrote contracts for others and formed companies of their own. And like lawyers across the ages they often hoped to be doing something more. Fortunately for the arts, many of these assertive and assured talents found that alternative — and respect — in patronage.

18 | Charles F. Osborn

A few years short of a century after Jake, Simon, and Max Kreielsheimer landed on the Seattle waterfront, a conservative lawyer of Irish descent with a penchant for work as steadfast as theirs sat surrounded by piles of files, bent over a desk only a few city blocks from the docks. Charles F. (Charlie) Osborn was calculating how at once to both multiply and give away the fortune that the family of Jewish brothers from Germany first helped accrue. Osborn, the first individual trustee of the Foundation, had met Leo Kreielsheimer years before Don Johnson, the second individual trustee, had graduated from law school. Later, Charlie would introduce Leo to Don. Both of Leo's individual trustees were men of considerable zest for their professions, yet both would learn to delight in performing the special services that Leo and Greye prescribed for them only. On many occasions they would prove again that lawyers are often a community's essential promoters of the fine arts, and in ways often more sophisticated even than those used to successfully defend the rights of Oscar Wilde's miner to the arms of the Venus de Milo.

Charles Osborn began helping Leo Kreielsheimer with his business affairs soon after graduating from Harvard Law School and joining the Bogle & Gates law firm in the 1940s. As a specialist in business, taxes, and estate planning, Osborn was Leo's lead lawyer at what was then the largest law firm in Seattle. While accompanying him on inspections of his Alaskan canneries Charles learned well his employer's inclinations, and in return Leo obviously liked Osborn's. This familiarity served them well through nearly thirty years of working together.

As a sportsman, Charles Osborn liked to play golf and climb mountains. As a lawyer he liked to work. By Don Johnson's description, "There are probably more elegant terms you could use, but Charlie was a workaholic. In the 108-year history of the firm no lawyer put in more years of service. When a sabbatical committee was formed in 1976 at the impetus of the younger partners, managing partner Stanley Long made Osborn the

Charles F. Osborn

chairman in an effort to inject some restraints on the sabbatical program. Nonetheless a generous sabbatical was adopted and from 1978 to his death in 1992 every partner that was eligible for sabbatical took it—except Charlie." Neither sabbatical nor retirement, of course, was appealing to Osborn, and after his mandatory retirement at age seventy, he continued to work not only with the Foundation but also at the firm with his old clients.

There are no reminiscences left by either the fish packer or his lawyer about how the idea of a foundation came forward, although it was likely some combination of inspiration, musing over taxes, and admiration for arts and artists. We may get a glimpse into both the working friendship and the contrasting tempers of Leo Kreielsheimer and Charles Osborn through a story told by Don Johnson. "Leo was a very pleasant man. He was short and had what I would call a 'pixyish' personality. There was a twinkle in his eye really, and with his pointed nose he could have played a character in a winter play—if you put a little makeup on him. Leo also had a sporting streak. He drove a yellow Corvette in the early 1960s. It was the sports car that young drag racers preferred, certainly not older gentleman investors who conventionally drove around in Cadillacs and Lincolns—long sedans that were most often black. Not Leo. One day about 1970 Leo had an appointment with me at Bogle & Gates to go over his investments. After greeting him in the reception room we headed down the hall to my office. On the way we walked by Charlie's office and the door was open. His was a large office and files were stacked everywhere so that to get to his chair Charlie often had to step around them. This was his normal working habit. At the time Charlie was sitting at his desk with his nose down in the papers

—he was a very earnest and serious worker—furiously writing out something. Poking his head through the door Leo intoned, 'Goood Mooorning Mr. OsBooorn.' Looking up at Leo, Charlie cleared his throat—he often did that—and cryptically replied 'Good morning Leo.' Leo retorted, 'My, what an *impeccable* office you keep!' Charlie then answered with some standard pleasantry like, 'Nice to see you Leo' and hastily returned to his writing. We then continued on to my office with Leo chuckling all the way. They were, of course, very close associates and friends but that they were a contrast in styles there is no doubt."

Although the Kreielsheimer Foundation was created upon Leo's death, it remained passive until Greye followed him in 1980, and brought the addition of her roughly equal part to the Foundation's reserve. An early although undated work sheet of Osborn's reveals as its title, "Possible principal distribution to 9-20-2000" and directly states his musings on how the Foundation's then $18,700,000 in assets might be divided. The few names included on this speculative list are for the most part those of the expected core institutions of local arts: the Museum, Opera, Symphony, and Ballet. But Osborn, the Notre Dame graduate, also penciled in arts scholarships for Spokane's Gonzaga University, and a "Beautification Arts Scholarship" for Seattle University. Leo's Alaska links are also represented in Osborn's early thoughts of what might be done, with a $1 million gift to the Anchorage Museum Foundation. (As was surveyed earlier in chapter 11 in a summary of all the Foundation's Alaska-bound gifts, Osborn's intuited million was in fact close to the actual amount given to the Anchorage Museum.)

There was, of course, no requirement for Charles Osborn to give it all quickly away and, as his few early choices demonstrated, his instincts were quite the opposite. Osborn's practice in the more parsimonious early years of the Foundation was ordinarily to disperse gifts from its invested account only to the minimum percentage required by tax laws. In total, the first trustee committed about $14.5 million in grants from 1981 to 1992. When compared to the crescendo of the Kreielsheimer giving that later reached in excess of $100 million, the restraint on Osborn's part can be seen in retrospect to have increased the bounty given through the hands of his successor.

In 1981 — the first year that gifts were distributed — Osborn gave a total of $94,000 and all of it to six institutions. Ten thousand dollars went to the Pacific Northwest Ballet for its production that year of *Swan Lake*. He continued to give regularly to the city's principal dance company and yet his accumulated gifts to PNB amounted to only $620,000 of the total $3,533,640 that the institution received from the Kreielsheimer Foundation. Charles Osborn also gave one of his first 1981 grants to the Intiman Theatre. In the Foundation catalog of awardees the amount is allocated for "acquisition and installation of costume[s], lighting, and sound equipment." Of the $60,000 Osborn gave the Theatre, the first gift was for $10,000. Don Johnson, his successor, sent another $3,297,940 on to Intiman, and that is a story with joyful turns that are nicely charted in chapter 3 by Jean Sherrard. The four other disbursements made in 1981 were to Virginia Mason Hospital, the Northwest School for Hearing Impaired Children, Forest Ridge School, and Business Volunteers for the Arts. Those gifts were for $4,000, $20,000, $35,000, and $15,000, respectively. In the last year of the Kreielsheimer Foundation, Don Johnson returned to some of Osborn's earliest recipients with new grants which, while generally modest, seemed to be given by the second trustee in a symbolic way as if to conclude the granting by drawing a circle that brought the first and last acts of the Foundation together. An example is the Northwest School of Hearing Impaired Children, to which in 2000 Johnson awarded an open grant of $25,000. These returns by Johnson to a number of Osborn's first interests were an expression of Johnson's appreciation for Osborn's choices as well as for his prudence. Often the "return grants" were also joyful surprises to the recipients.

For the fiscal year 1981–82, Osborn more than doubled the Foundation's giving — to $211,500. Most of this was distributed to twenty-six new applicants, and so by later standards the grants were still generally modest ones. Similarly, the trustee shared modesty for the work of the Foundation; it was his practice to regularly append to the awards he gave notes to the winners explaining, "The Kreielsheimer family has always shunned publicity and continues to do so. It is the wish of the family that no publicity be given to the gift and that only a minimum appropriate recognition be given as may be necessary for recordkeeping." In 1981–82 a quarter of the help distributed — $50,000 — went to Whitman College for expansion of its Hall of Music. The other "whit" on the dry side of Washington State, Whitworth College in Spokane, received $5,000 for restoration of its grand piano.*

With one exception, the grants given during fiscal year 1982–83 are in line with the Foundation's established mission of support for arts and education — and mostly the former. Pacific Northwest Ballet was given $15,000 support for the production of *Chaconne*, a work choreographed by Balanchine. Western Washington University purchased new practice pianos with a $3,000 gift, the Seattle Symphony Orchestra received $10,000 in support, and Northwest School of the Arts was able to equip their ceramics studio with a $10,000 donation. The one exception to this elevation of the arts was the gift given to what was then still Seattle's favorite charity, the Children's Orthopedic Hospital. It received $17,500 for the purchase of equipment that is not described. But by far the largest disbursement was for what soon became known as the "Kreielsheimer Block," or more familiarly, the K block.

In the Foundation's IRS report for 1983 the K block is still hopefully called the "Seattle Art Museum site." There, Charles Osborn invested what was for him at the time a whopping total disbursement of $2,269,161. This early interest in land and what might be built upon it became very much a Kreielsheimer theme. Rarely did either of the Foundation's individual trustees focus on funding the operating expenses of arts institutions. Don Johnson explains, "We thought that those should be provided by sources normally available in the community." On occasion both Osborn and Johnson did release substantial funding for special projects, including worthy programs that might otherwise not be presented. But the greatest work of the Kreielsheimer legacy went to support two major areas: first, the creation and sustenance of endowments, and then toward the building of several of the region's grandest halls and homes for the arts. Johnson notes, "Many of these probably could not have been built without Kreielsheimer support. But, having said that, they could not have happened without community support as well. Together we helped reform the old order in which art organizations typically lived from hand to mouth and day to day and never got enough money to build a wooden shed let alone a concert hall."

* This was most likely the Baldwin that author Paul Dorpat remembers accompanied the school choir when he was a member in the early 1960s.

On more than one occasion either trustee could have easily grabbed at the exhilarating experience of giving it all away in a few days—a philanthropic splurge. There were certainly many worthy applicants. And inevitably, perhaps, the uncertainties and exasperation connected with trying to raise millions for a big project did inspire enthused critics to recommend just such a quick fix, envisioning Kreielsheimer opening its tap and painlessly filling every need. In this regard the robustly good-natured Don Johnson's exasperation over the quick call of a naive critic offers a glance into the way the public's simple notions of the power of philanthropy are often blind to the complexities of responsible gift-giving. After Osborn's passing, a *Seattle Weekly* critic in effect stated, as Johnson recalls it, "that with one stroke of the pen the trustee could have paid for a Symphony Hall and all the anxious fund-raising would have been over." It still rankles Johnson when he recalls that article. "I felt constrained to defend Charlie because this article came out six or eight months after he died and he wasn't there to defend himself. I wrote a letter for publication in the *Weekly* and called my friend David Brewster, the *Weekly*'s editor, explaining that if Charlie had done that it would have been a very poor administration of the assets that were entrusted to him. David published the rather long letter in full. With two or three of those kinds of gifts there wouldn't be a story to tell aside from a fancy building here or there. The Kreielsheimer fund was not created to be quickly disposed in two or three projects."

Such a quick fix would also have violated the Foundation's prudent policy that private funds should be matched or exceeded by other contributions, including public funds. Don Johnson explains, "In respect to the concert hall, that meant funds appropriated by the Legislature, by King County, the City of Seattle, and major gifts by capable private philanthropists—and contributions by everyday folks giving $50 and $100 checks. You put all those things together and you can do it. In my opinion—and I didn't discuss this with Charlie but I believe he would agree—if nobody else wants to do it, it isn't worth doing. While that is simplistic and not true in every instance, it is true in many. We wanted the community involved, and as matters turned out the concert hall was built by the community through a great public-private partnership. McCaw Hall is another successful example of this approach."

19 | Donald L. Johnson

On the night of August 31, 1992, Charles F. Osborn lost his battle with cancer. Six years earlier, after completing a round of therapy, Osborn told Melinda Bargreen that his doctor fully expected him to see the century out "unless I get hit by a truck." Less than three months before Osborn's death Johnson found him collapsed in the Two Union Square lobby. "I was coming back from a meeting and I heard the Medic 1 sirens but thought nothing of it. When I went into the lobby there were two medics helping Charlie, but they couldn't get him to sit comfortably in a chair. I asked, 'May I call Harriet?' But he stoically replied, 'Oh no, that isn't necessary.' Well it was."

After Osborn's passing at the end of August 1992, Don Johnson became the new individual trustee on September 1, 1992, thirty-five years to the day after he had come to work for Bogle & Gates on September 1, 1957, as a young lawyer out of law school. He recalls, "With the other young lawyers I was required to attend a weekly meeting at 8 a.m. every Friday morning presided over by a then-young partner of the firm named Charles F. Osborn. We were each asked to tell a story about what was interesting in our practice the previous week, in a school setting we all referred to as 'Osborn Tech.' Charlie added this instruction to his normal duties because he was such a believer in professional excellence."

Don Johnson was evidently a good student, for Osborn selected him in the 1960s to help Leo Kreielsheimer acquire investment properties. Johnson recalls, "I enjoyed working with Leo Kreielsheimer a great deal and I know Charlie did too. The three of us had a delightful relationship. At some point (and my recollection is hazy) Charlie mentioned that Leo had designated me as a backup individual trustee. But in those days we were all younger and I didn't have any illusions of becoming the Kreielsheimer trustee, and I am sure Charlie felt that he would probably be the one who would do this for the full twenty-five years. One always wants to think there is going to be a happy ending to these things but there wasn't. We all tend to feel we are

Donald L. Johnson

immortal until in later life we realize that we aren't. There was a sense, especially after Charlie's collapse in the summer of the year he died, that he wasn't going to recover this time. I knew then that I had to start focusing on the Foundation. However, I don't think I had any real discussion with Charlie about running it. He was very conservative and one of the smartest lawyers with respect to sensible investments. I knew about some of the Foundation's projects and at that time there really were not that many."

After he became familiar with details that were formerly Charles Osborn's concerns Don Johnson decided to care for them full time. "I concluded quickly that my first obligation was to devote my energies to trying to carry out Leo and Greye Kreielsheimer's trust and to discharge it as well as I possibly could. It was an ethical matter, and it wasn't very long before I became the de-facto full-time trustee. Increasingly I passed my law practice over to younger lawyers in the office." As trustee, Johnson moved to a small office in Bogle & Gates's elegant quarters at Two Union Square, and his many friends at the firm also helped him through the transition. He was given continued use of the firm's technical and clerical services, and the part-time help of a legal secretary—all on a "pass-through" cost basis. Johnson held many meetings with local art leaders in the firm's conference rooms. By his description, "It worked just beautifully."

The changes wrought for Don Johnson by dint of his switch from business lawyer to trustee were by his own description "not that great, because the vast majority of the Foundation's recipients were based in or near Seattle, and after all, at the age of sixty-two I wasn't born yesterday." Indeed, Bogle & Gates had long been a familiar stage for the financial and political play of the community's leaders. Still, as Foundation trustee,

Johnson would be in frequent contact with the Rubinsteins, Gerberdings, Wrights, Benaroyas, Strouns, and more — all the major philanthropists and leaders of Seattle's increasingly large arts milieu. Fortunately for both the Foundation and its new trustee these contacts with community shakers were almost always both effective and congenial.

The first call for Don Johnson was to get to know better the persons from whom Charles Osborn had been suddenly separated. Johnson observed, "I spent much time meeting them in the fall of 1992. Actually it was a very intense experience having people come and ask, 'What are you thinking? What are you going to do?' and giving them a feeling of security that the world was not ending. I made a decision, probably before Charlie died but formally afterward, that I was not going to be running around stopping things because I might have a little different view of it. If there was a project that was in process I would rarely interfere."

Johnson further observed, "I grew up in this town and I love it and you know I've also got a bunch of artists in my family. You see I have never thought of this job as being overwhelming or intimidating. But when you look at the fact that in 1992 the assets were about $50 million and that it was basically my responsibility as the individual trustee to dispose of this money — well, it was clear to me that if I was going to do the job I should not do it halfway but rather devote my full time to it. Still, in the beginning I had some time. There were then eight years more to go and I certainly wasn't going to start giving away 'X percent' of the money in the next month or quarter just to go through the motions. What I did first was study. And one of the first big things that emerged was the need to decide on whether or not to hold on to the K block for a new symphony concert hall."*

The round table in the Kreielsheimer conference room in the Century Building was the setting for many meetings with local arts groups, and Don Johnson thought of the table itself as a metaphor for their joined work of extending the "circle of arts." The pleasant task of enlarging the circle of arts also created a growing circle of friends for the gregarious Johnson. In both principle and practice the Kreielsheimer Foundation supported many programs and many arts. "It soon became apparent to me that the focus

* See also chapter 5 of this book.

was art and not on one kind of art. I would try to spread it around to arts in a broad sense."

This call for variety sometimes meant rescuing endangered programs. "If it came to a point where I had to decide between two groups that were each equally meritorious in their own way I would ordinarily choose the one in greatest need. The choice would not be made because it was this sort of art or that. I mean, I am a music person — and, for example by her own admission, the great philanthropist Virginia Wright is a visual person, and so on. Both the musical and the visual arts are, of course, richly represented in the list of Kreielsheimer recipients. While I am a fan of ballet and the dancing of Patricia Barker and the Pacific Northwest Ballet, I did not presume to therefore dismiss the choreography of Mark Morris. Although modern dance does not touch me like, say, *Swan Lake*, I still recognize the genius of Morris. Certainly the way I read the Kreielsheimer will is that it emphasizes a broad support for the visual and performing arts."

Except for one momentary concern already noted above that he might need other opportunities beyond the arts to effectively disperse the millions that were left in the Foundation's account as it approached its eleventh hour, Don Johnson routinely found plenty of worthy applications coming from the circle of arts. "Most philanthropic scholars will tell you that of all the good causes the arts is one of the most neglected. The arts are somehow the last among equals. When the budgets are cut in Olympia the arts are the first to suffer and the last to participate in good times. For the Foundation that made it all the more compelling in its mission to try to help fill that gap."

Trustee Touchstones

Work with the Foundation brought touchstones for both trustees—
moments and associations that shone with extra illumination. For Don
Johnson, mementos of some of these are kept near at hand. Besides the
photographs on the walls and shelves around him—snapshots usually—
of dedications and other cherished moments connected with Kreielsheimer
grants, there are letters that are valued for many reasons. These are kept in
a file that has no name, probably because the contents are often so personal
that they seem to ask for a cover that calls no attention. There is a hand-
written letter, for instance, from past University of Washington President
Richard McCormick. For Johnson it is not that the message is earthshak-
ing, but that it is "so well and simply phrased, a model of elegant writing."
Johnson confides, "It is a quality to be earnestly hoped for in lawyers who
are too often inclined to riddle even their friendly conversations with legal-
istic jargon."

The file also includes a congratulatory letter from Bagley Wright on
the addition of the Leo K. wing to the Seattle Repertory Theatre. Its
founder reminisces that while it was once his greatest passion he still has a
soft spot for it. Another letter folded in the nameless but cherished file is
from Stephen Wadsworth, the renowned director of both opera and theatre
(including the 2001 and 2005 Ring productions at the Seattle Opera). It
summarizes the Kreielsheimer largess with candor: "Now here's a heartfelt
thank you for your sponsorship of *Don Juan*. What an honor to have had
the support, over these past several years, of you and the Kreielsheimer
Foundation. Your generosity is a moving force in my work for this community—clearly it makes that work possible, but the GIVING is the inspiring
thing."

The greatest influences upon both trustees came directly from Leo and
Greye Kreielsheimer's love for the region's best performing groups like the
opera and the ballet. Don Johnson especially enjoys opera, and Perry
Lorenzo, Seattle Opera's director of education, routinely nourished and

informed this affection. Speight Jenkins, the Opera's director, describes him as "the best." Always delighted with Lorenzo's lectures on the operas performed by Seattle Opera, in 1996 Johnson gave an unsolicited $50,000 to the Opera marked for his work. Few other Foundation grants were given with such firsthand or direct motivation.

Charles Osborn sometimes liked to cross the mountains with his giving. Otherwise the Cascades were a barrier that was barely bridged, for the Foundation was created to support arts "in the Northwest, and particularly in Western Washington." As noted earlier, Johnson did not renew Osborn's early interest in arts programs at Gonzaga University in Spokane. Charles Osborn was also enamored with the art of the Western artist John Clymer who was born and raised in Ellensburg and best known for his cover illustrations for the *Saturday Evening Post* and his oils depicting Western themes. Osborn gave a series of grants totaling $155,000 to the modest Clymer Museum in Ellensburg.

In the networking that was often a necessary prelude to making granting decisions there were a few leaders in the Northwest arts that Don Johnson trusted to be both smart and spirited. Don has long admired local philanthropists Sam and Gladys Rubinstein who were among those who could scrutinize projects with prudence and passion at the same time. Johnson's $100,000 gift to the Seattle Chamber Music Festival was given in honor of the Rubinsteins, the Festival's perennial supporters. Sam Rubinstein was also involved in the decision of the Foundation to give major support to ACT Theatre in its move from a familiar but limiting venue on lower Queen Anne to the restored Eagles Auditorium. At its opening, Johnson commented to Rubinstein, "This is a historic building of the sort hard to find north of San Francisco." In effect, supporting the ACT move would also help save the landmark. Johnson, a retired business lawyer, confesses, "This is the kind of circumstance that motivates me to support the project. I am sort of a real-estate freak."

Long before he assumed the duties of the Foundation as its individual trustee Don Johnson worked with the Rubinsteins when he helped them find a suitable home. After choosing their swank unit near Kerry Park on the south slope of Queen Anne Hill, Johnson recalls that the couple responded to the condominium's rule against pets by asking that the restriction be repealed as a condition for moving in. The persuasive couple soon took occupancy with their dog Sockeye. Johnson notes, "That may be the first condominium development where the buyer of one unit rewrote the rules." On another occasion, when Johnson commented to Sam Rubinstein how a possible estate planning decision would result in more taxes for his estate, Rubinstein replied, "Well, so what." It was an unexpected response and Johnson admired it. "I love the generosity implicit in that. 'Okay, if I've got to pay taxes, I've got to pay taxes. So what. I'm not going to worry about it.' It displayed his generous attitude toward the community. He's a great guy—a story in himself."

The parts played by women are notable both in Don Johnson's life and in his duties as trustee. The woman who first nurtured him with the sensitivities needed to negotiate the world of the arts and to deal with artists was his mother, Edith Johnson. The trustee is quick to follow that up with, "I will tell you a personal story. My mother was an artist." And he proudly points to the examples of her work displayed on the shelves and walls of his office. Included among examples of his mother's art that Don Johnson kept near his desk is a detail of the Pike Place Market that reveals a skilled handling of the earth-tone coloring and identifying lines of the Northwest School, especially of Mark Tobey's own market sketchbook. "I brought them down just for this purpose—to show people in the arts. You can see it and seeing it is worth a thousand words. Edith did a number of paintings of the Market. She loved it. She would take me down there when I was a little kid. Of course our family purchased one of the Market tiles for her. After my brother Roger and I were raised she went back to

Edith Johnson working on sculpture art, ca. 1958

154

The Market by Edith Johnson

study at the University of Washington and completed the degree in fine arts she had started before she got married."

With the considerable nurturing of his artistic mother, Don Johnson's distaff influences continued with his wife, Dottie, and three daughters, all of whom took a special interest in the arts. By the time he became trustee Johnson had a considerable head start in transcending centuries-old gender bias. He was, it seems, especially receptive to their advice, a quality that was timely considering the number of women with whom he happily worked and learned.

Two Gypsies by Edith Johnson

Johnson took charge of Foundation giving at a time when the Opera, the Seattle Symphony, and the Seattle Repertory Theatre were all either in the ministering hands of women or were about to be. For instance, Deborah Card began her tenure as chief administrator of the Symphony in late 1992, only a few months after Johnson became trustee. From their work together through the campaign for a new concert hall, as well as in the development of special-program support both for the Symphony and for the Soundbridge Learning Center, Johnson spontaneously places her in his "top ten." Kathy Magiera, Seattle Opera's late dynamic director, is also up there. Johnson explains, "Kathy came to the Opera in 1991, about six months before I became the trustee.

Don and Dottie Johnson at the dedication of McCaw Hall

She had been told the funding experts said that it would take at least three years to get the Opera turned around. She said, 'I can do it in eighteen months,' and she did. To be so charming and yet at the same time to be a tough administrator — well, it was too good to be true, but it was true. Of course she had both business and managerial training as well as training in the arts."

A listing of the feminine influences on the second trustee quickly exceeds ten, and the chronicle may continue by first noting that Don Johnson's respect for Seattle Center Director Virginia Anderson has already been sketched earlier in this book. Johnson describes the director of the Seattle Center as an "incredible doer, straight shooter, and a good friend. Virginia is easily one of the most significant people in the Seattle community." He describes Laura Penn as "the Kathy Magiera and Deborah Card for Intiman Theater. I worked with her especially for rehearsal and endowment support." Community philanthropist Ann Ramsay-Jenkins is a "special friend and a sparkplug. Her passionate interest in both the Seattle Repertory Theatre and the Book-It Theatre have meant a lot to their respective success." Susan Trapnell, the longtime managing director of ACT, engineer of its move to Kreielsheimer Place, and past chairman of the Seattle Arts Commission, Johnson describes as having "that rare overview that goes beyond even her own projects." Linda Hartzell, the "genius of the Seattle Children's Theatre" also taught Don and Dottie's youngest daughter Karin at Lakeside School. To Johnson, philanthropist Virginia Wright is both the primary mover of the visual arts in the community and "a story unto herself." He describes Melissa Hines, for years the soldier holding the Empty Space Theater together, by the reception she got at the Seattle Asian Art Museum on the occasion of winning the Corporate Council for the Arts/ArtsFund's

Unsung Hero Award for Perseverance and Dedication in the Arts. "Everyone stood up and cheered. *Everybody*, not just the theater people!"

The list of modern distaff influences also includes Jane Lang Davis. In Johnson's estimation she is "one of the great philanthropists in Seattle with joi de vivre and the spirit to do it." Philanthropist Ida Cole is characterized as a "If you are going to do it then I'll help out person. For the Intiman Theatre we did a $1 million challenge grant and Ida came through with a $750,000 match. I mean just like that!" Another "strong supporter of the arts" whom Don Johnson consulted for her overview of local arts was Deanna Oppenheimer, a senior officer at Washington Mutual Bank. Like the others just noted, Louise Kincaid at the Northwest Chamber Orchestra took hold of her stewardship in September 1992 and was the Orchestra's dedicated administrator until the spring of 2002. In a 1997 article titled "Women Are Powers on Arts Scene" by *Seattle Times* critic Melinda Bargreen, Kincaid's appreciation for the Foundation is noted. "The past three years also have brought important support from the Kreielsheimer Foundation, whose money is not only a leverage (employed as a 'challenge grant') but also a stamp of approval in the donor community that has had what Kincaid calls 'immeasurable effect.' "

Melinda Bargreen herself gave encouragement with her sympathetic *Seattle Times* reports on productions and projects to which the Foundation had lent a hand. Johnson notes, "If I wanted to get a message to the community one of the few ways was with a story through the *Times* or the *P-I*." Melinda Bargreen was especially appreciated and the trustee often went to her first. Don Johnson was touched by the way she impressed the sometimes impassive Charlie Osborn. Bargreen's own term for Osborn was "feisty." As for her handling of his time as trustee, Johnson notes, "I don't remember her distorting in any significant way the substance of what I might have shared with her. That is tough to do even if you try. I admire her." In turn, in her 1996 review of the "arts boom" Bargreen pegs Don Johnson's prudent mode of operation. "He chose not to lavish the Foundation's assets on a single project, as many have urged him to do. Such a move would violate Leo Kreielsheimer's wishes, but Johnson also knows he can do more good by providing an incentive for other donors. Look at any important project and Kreielsheimer money is there. Because the money is bestowed so carefully, it has become a valued imprimatur, a stamp

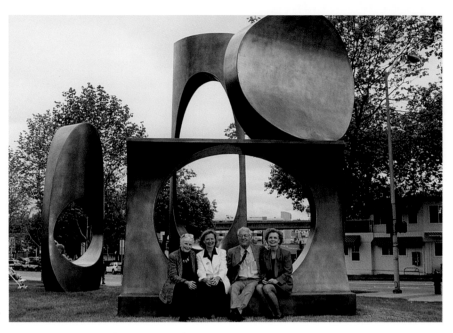

Left to right: Doris Chase, Pam Schell, Don Johnson, and Virginia Anderson at the 1999 dedication of Chase's *Moon Gates* in the Sculpture Garden at Seattle Center

of approval — and frequently a lifesaver." The Johnson-Bargreen connection once actually took wing when, together with Seattle Opera's general director Speight Jenkins, the trio soared above the Opera House stage in a test flight of the horses used in the "Ride of the Valkyries" scene of the Opera's 1996 production of Wagner's *Ring*. The critic's "trepidation" over being strapped to a flying fiberglass horse was calmed considerably once she realized that Don Johnson would be flying beside her. "They weren't going to drop Don Johnson, co-trustee and decision-maker for the Kreielsheimer Foundation, whose largesse has significantly helped Seattle Opera." (Bargreen implies that dropping a journalist might be another thing.)

Among the snapshots and art standing on the shelf beside Johnson's desk is a group photograph of Doris Chase, Virginia Anderson, Pam Schell, and himself. The occasion is the June 23, 1999, dedication of the Doris Chase sculpture in the Sculpture Garden near the base of the Space Needle at Seattle Center. Titled *Moon Gates*, the sculpture was, in major part, supported by the Foundation, a reflection of the admiration Don and Dottie Johnson had held for her work since the 1960s. Of the "gracious" Pam Schell, Johnson notes, "She is one of my heroines. Pam worked extremely hard on everything, including her husband's mayoral duties, and would

Left to right: Don Johnson, Sam Rubinstein, Gerry Tsutakawa, and Jack Benaroya, with the newly finished *Urban Peace Circle*

show up repeatedly at events he was unable to attend. She has a special love of the Intiman Theatre and the Pike Place Market as well."

The Kreielsheimer contributions made to the community by support of the work of the many talented members of the Tsutakawa family began with Charles Osborn's 1989 gift of the George Tsutakawa sculpture, entitled *Centennial Fountain*, to Seattle University. Don Johnson also granted $250,000 to pay for the cost of moving and replacing the widely admired George Tsutakawa work entitled *Fountain of Wisdom* from its position on the Fifth Avenue side of the old downtown Seattle Public Library to its new place at the southwest corner of the new Seattle Central Library on the Fourth Avenue level. Two works by Gerard "Gerry" Tsutakawa were funded in part by the Foundation. The artist's *Urban Peace Circle* is a work promoted by the Stop the Violence Group and made from fused handgun metal. It is mounted in the park created atop the Interstate 90 Highway lid on the Rainier Valley side of the Mount Baker Tunnel. Gerry Tsutakawa's welded-bronze fountain on the Seattle Center campus just south of Intiman Theater was installed in October 2000. The name *Seseragi* in its title, meaning "murmuring waters," is realized by two streams that merge together. Finally, when the Garfield High School Orchestra was ready to cancel its 1997 trip to Europe, the Foundation came forward and made up the difference. Led by Marcus Tsutakawa, this European tour included a second-place finish in the internationally renowned Vienna Youth and Music Festival. The entire Tsutakawa family has been one of the real treasures of Northwest art for over seventy-five years.

Part V

Epilogue

21 | Endowments and Remainders

The Kreielsheimer Foundation neither advertised for applications nor tailored the proposals it received. However, on occasion the individual trustees — Osborn and Johnson — did use their unique status to share reflections on how money that was about to be delivered to their choices might be used. This activism became fairly commonplace near the end, as Don Johnson directed many large grants toward endowments, and thereby helped secure the chances for future vitality for many groups it had already helped, often in a variety of ways. These latter-day contributions also gave him a sensible means of averting a potential embarrassment of riches as the Foundation approached its eleventh hour.

The second trustee made public the coming shift in the Foundation's emphasis from capital projects to endowments in a conversation with Melinda Bargreen in 1996. "You can build a beautiful building, and then fall flat if you can't maintain and manage it properly." The *Times* critic concluded correctly, since the Foundation then had only four years more to disburse its assets, that it would likely play an important role in funding future endowments for the arts. Also by 1996 Johnson was midway through his eight-year term and he felt that he "knew the territory" after studying it for four years. Given the bullish growth of the Foundation's investments, Johnson wondered if he might need to go beyond the arts. "When we got to the point where the available money was getting 'real' — toward the last two or three years — I knew that there were, of course, many attractive candidates that were not really in the arts. Consequently, the Foundation, joined by the attorney general, obtained a declaratory judgment, that — to oversimplify — it would be in substantial compliance with the donors' intent if we gave at least half of the Foundation funds to the arts." But nothing came of this idea of adjusting the Foundation's borders. Johnson's increasing desire to both start and strengthen endowments was one big reason to withdraw from any new expansion. Instead on January 1, 1999, Johnson did the opposite. He quit taking applications.

"We indicated that we would no longer accept unsolicited requests. While we did not shut the door to new things, we expected to find them in a field that we were by then already very familiar with. We felt that we knew pretty much where the most deserving needs were."

Probably the most dramatic revelation of the Foundation's new emphasis on endowments occurred on the evening of May 19, 1997, at a Seattle Repertory Theatre event billed as "Inspecting Dan: The Sullivan Chronicles." The occasion was a farewell for the Rep's longtime artistic director Dan Sullivan. With actress Amy Irving and playwright Wendy Wasserstein performing as co-emcees, one of the evening's highlights was a histrionic presentation that brought trustee Don Johnson to the stage. *Seattle Times* theater critic Misha Berson reported, "Bidding adieu after seventeen years at the Rep's helm, Sullivan left a little something behind: a surprise $1 million gift from the Kreielsheimer Foundation establishing a new Daniel Sullivan Artistic Development Fund. The grant, announced by Kreielsheimer co-trustee Donald L. Johnson, must be matched with another million dollars in contributions over the next four years." The actual on-stage act of giving created its own comic scene. As Johnson prepared to hand over to Sullivan the first installment, a $250,000 check, the Rep's Managing Director Ben Moore jumped on stage and grabbed it shouting, "Hand me that check." Feigning an uncharacteristic subdued and quiet manner, Sullivan meekly handed over the check. When matched, the Sullivan fund is expected to generate a yearly income of about $50,000 in perpetuity.

Laura Penn, the managing director of the Intiman Theatre, another arts organization richly endowed by the Foundation, made it clear that the endowments distributed by Don Johnson are gifts to the entire arts community. "We cannot touch the principal of this fund for any reason. This isn't a safety net in that way. . . . If for some reason we should not be around, this endowment would go to another theater. It wouldn't save us because that's not what he's in the business of doing. It's a commitment to the long-term health of the Seattle arts community, and a reminder that the world is bigger than us."

And also smaller. Johnson makes the point, "But I'm not just interested in the big groups." A good percentage of the Foundation's largess — about $11 million — has been given for the endowments of smaller arts organizations like the Seattle Chamber Music Festival ($160,720), the Seattle Youth Symphony ($267,860) and Artist Trust ($160,720). These irregular amounts came about as a function of "emptying the till on a percentage-distribution basis upon closure of the Foundation." So, for instance, the $100,000 endowment granted to the Bellevue Philharmonic Orchestra had another $7,140 added upon closure for an odd total of $107,140.

While exhilarating, the general bounty of the last grants also triggered a nostalgic reflection in the last trustee. Don Johnson reflected, "You and I know good people who have spent their entire lives working in businesses, professions, or other types of employment that are not lucrative and they are lucky if they have perhaps $50,000 to give to mankind when they are ready to pass on. And I sat there and routinely wrote checks for $50,000 or much more! I was a kid during the Depression, and although our family was relatively fortunate, I saw how the poverty affected everybody. Fifty thousand dollars is a lot of money. It is somebody's life. So I could not give Kreielsheimer grants without reflecting how 'hard-earned' even modest grants were for most people."

That the "winners" in arts fund-raising are ordinarily already proven ones may seem to create something resembling a celebrity system of the worthy. However, every artist and arts group obviously has to start somewhere and most have had to get some breaks. With the arts, one of the oldest clichés of capital — that one has to have money in the bank in order to get money from a bank — does not always apply. But at the other end of this tale every artist and arts group who wants to continue making art — and most importantly that means owning the time to make it — had better have money in the bank, or a stream of support that is some combination of sales and donations. For those who do not, making art is a hard life, and few artists would give any currency to the notion that the art of a starving artist is the better for it. Rather there is an understandable urge to generate art within a sturdy armature of support. For the bigger arts organizations like the Symphony, the Art Museum, the Ballet, and the Opera, which support many professionals, endowments are a necessity. Without endowments they are tied to a fiscal clock that always returns to the annual ritual on the first day of the fiscal year of once again commencing the begging — often inspired begging but still begging.

22 | Return to Mercer Street

The Kreielsheimer Promenade is situated at the base of the west-facing glass wall of McCaw Hall, both inside and outside it, and the transparent divider flows like the hem of a loose skirt or the French curves of a viola d'amore. The Promenade reaches west over moving sheets of water to the reflecting east wall of the Phelps Center. The name of the Foundation and credit to it are elegantly written on this refurbished facade of the Pacific Northwest Ballet's facility. Nearby, embedded in a granite rock, is a plaque that reads:

> As stewards and leaders, initially Charles F. Osborn and later Donald L. Johnson guided the generous and invaluable work of the Kreielsheimer Foundation during its 25-year history from 1975 to 2000. The legacy of the Foundation's visionary and strategic giving of more than $100 million can be seen in the beauty and vibrancy of the region's arts and educational institutions. Of the foregoing, over $53 million has been given to the City of Seattle and Seattle Center Foundation and to other recipients operating on or associated with this 74-acre Seattle Center campus in support of capital, endowment, operational, and other expenses. These include significant Kreielsheimer grants to: Marion Oliver McCaw Hall, Seattle Opera, Seattle Symphony, Pacific Northwest Ballet, Seattle Center Foundation, Seattle Center Theatre District, Seattle Repertory Theatre, Intiman Theatre, Seattle Children's Theatre, Pacific Science Center, KCTS, ArtsFund, Book-It Theatre, Bumbershoot, Doris Chase *Moon Gates*, Gerard Tsutakawa *Fountain of Seseragi*, International Music Festival of Seattle Center, Seattle Center Academy, Seattle Chamber Music Festival, and the Children's Museum. The City of Seattle and Seattle Center express the heartfelt appreciation of the citizens of our community for this gracious support.
>
> [Signed] Greg Nickels, Mayor; Virginia Anderson, Seattle Center Director, June 2003.

Plaque in granite rock at Seattle Center

In the late winter of 2003 Don Johnson took a last hard-hat tour of McCaw Hall and the Kreielsheimer Promenade. The trustee's nervous anticipation was soon dispelled by the overall impression of the openness and vast elegance of the place, even though it was then still a work in progress. The Promenade's great transparent overhead scrims, designed by Leni Schwendinger to reflect an array of projected colors, were not yet in place but the stately row of columns that would hold and extend them from the great glass wall were.

The Promenade seemed to speak to Johnson's regard for music. After his family, opera may be his first love. "My personal favorite has become Wagner's work, especially the "Ring." It just melts me. Do you know the "Liebestod" aria from *Tristan und Isolde*? Perhaps the greatest live music I have ever heard was Jane Eaglen singing the "Liebestod" in Benaroya Hall at an Opera benefit performance in August 1999. It just broke me up." Very likely he will hear it again in McCaw Hall. Wagner's *Parsifal* was the first opera scheduled for the McCaw Hall in the late summer of 2003, and at this writing the Ring scheduled for August 2005 was recently performed to rave reviews.

While the Kreielsheimer Promenade is also a partial answer to what some have called the "Mercer Street mess," Don Johnson recalls what he learned earlier from visiting planners hired by Seattle Center to give suggestions on how to improve its built environment. They unanimously reported to Virginia Anderson, in effect, that "as we drove down Mercer Street we passed the greatest assembly of visual and performing arts organizations north of San Francisco and west of Chicago and yet you wouldn't know it!"

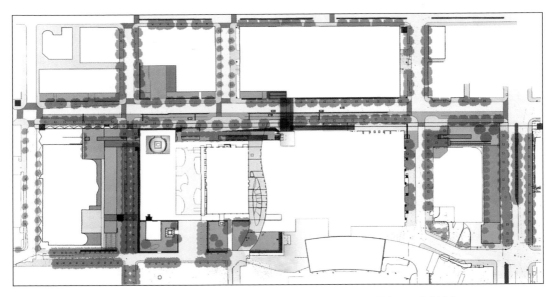

Conceptual Site Plan of Seattle Center's "Theatre District," 2001

Why? The 1962 World's Fair put a Chinese wall around Seattle Center to control payment for entry to the fairgrounds, and everything was constructed to face inward toward the middle of the fair site.

Virginia Anderson has undertaken studies of possible improvements to the Mercer Street area between Warren Avenue North and Fifth Avenue North, an area designated by the planners as the Seattle Center Theater District. Concepts under consideration are reflected in the Seattle Center Theater District Site Plan reproduced here. From the Kreielsheimer Promenade one can look on a diagonal across Mercer Street to the K Block, which, at this writing, floats like an iceberg of possibility, the mass of its hoped-for improvements still submerged beneath the parking lot and small park that cover it. The grove of cherry trees that decorates its one modestly landscaped corner (where once the Royal Crown Cola's modern bottling plant stood at Third Avenue North) is a hint of what Mercer Street might become should the Foundation's and Seattle Center's hopes for it be fulfilled. An L-shaped piece of the K block that extends thirty-eight feet deep along Mercer Street between Second Avenue North and Third Avenue North, and reaches another fifty feet up Second Avenue makes up the one-third of the K block given to Seattle Center for a park.

Anderson explains, "The L-shaped piece is meant to enhance the notion that the Theater District would be developed along both sides of

Mercer Street, south and north." Don Johnson also imagines along Mercer Street a continuation of the elegant design qualities that were brought to the Kreielsheimer Promenade by the celebrated landscape architect Kathryn Gustafson. And in Johnson's vision both the Bagley Wright Theatre and the Intiman Theatre's home in the old Playhouse would be opened or presented to Mercer Street. The remaining two-thirds of the K block are reserved for a future Opera Center — a facility designed to support the work of the Seattle Opera as the Phelps Center provides for Pacific Northwest Ballet.

The Kreielsheimer Remainder Foundation was formed by Johnson in part to hold in trust some funds which, when the time came, might help transform the jumble along Mercer Street into an avenue that lends significance to the distinguished arts institutions built beside it. With the help of a group of Kreielsheimer challenge grants given in 2000, collectively exceeding $8 million, the Seattle Center Foundation hopes to campaign for and ultimately to build a coherent Theater District along Mercer Street. Whether this elegant dream ultimately becomes a reality or is dispelled depends upon decisions yet to be made by Seattle's mayor and City Council, and upon sufficient public-private partnership support needed to match the Kreielsheimer challenge grants before the expiration dates of those grants in the year 2010.

Much had changed in the few years between the dedications of Benaroya and McCaw halls. The charmed economics of the 1990s became history in early 2001, and after September 11 appeared like a lost Golden Age as well. The economy dropped at a moment that depressed both the private and public sides engaged in the final funding for McCaw Hall. The county and the state failed to meet their pledges on time and may take years to pay. Greg Nickels, the city's new mayor, over the objections of several members of the City Council, made a special bridge loan of $27.8 million to insure that McCaw Hall would be finished on time.

Another casualty of the harder times was some of the old collegiality between the major arts organizations, which had included the tacit agreement not to launch competing capital campaigns but to take turns. The abundant reach of the Seattle Symphony endowment campaign had already overlapped the fund-raising work for McCaw Hall. But an example closer to the Center involved the two principal players in the McCaw Hall campaign: the Opera and the Ballet. In the spring of 2002, while the struggle to find the remaining funds for McCaw Hall was still continuing, both the Opera and the Center were startled when Pacific Northwest Ballet began a $5 million capital campaign to build a new teaching facility in Bellevue. Seattle Center Director Virginia Anderson, a master of diplomacy, put the best construction on this dicey scene in an interview with *Post-Intelligencer* music critic R. M. Campbell: "We didn't know the scope of the project until the Ballet made its public announcement. I don't know the impact of this campaign on McCaw Hall. Fund-raising is as much art as science. The difference between the Symphony's endowment campaign and the Ballet's is that the Symphony is not a partner in McCaw Hall and PNB is. However, I understand the donor that made the lead gift ($1 million over three years) would not have given to the McCaw Hall campaign. The fund-raising climate is very different now. Perhaps it is a sign of urban growth that we have multiple projects going at one time."

Years earlier the philosophical and visionary Virginia Anderson had advised and impressed Don Johnson, saying, "Don, I'm an incrementalist." It was, of course, easier to persevere step-by-step when the Kreielsheimer Foundation was still at hand to help with the walking. Maestro Gerard Schwarz expressed this loss at the Symphony's luncheon honoring Don Johnson and the Foundation on its closing. "I'm very sad. Here is a foundation whose trustees have cared deeply about the arts, and the results have been quite remarkable. There isn't an equivalent foundation to replace them, and I feel we don't have that partner who has been with us for so long." To Don Johnson it was an uncanny coincidence that the Seattle arts scene took a downward turn soon after the Foundation closed its door. Practically everyone involved would have to learn how to make difficult steps backward.

A short sketch of recent Seattle arts history reveals that such cyclical evolutions of fortune are more commonplace than rare. For instance, the reversals of thirty and more years ago during the Boeing Recession prefigured those of 2000 and beyond. The fortunes of Seattle Center itself, the former Fair site, seemed very much in doubt following the initial cultural catapult of Century 21. The loss of Boeing's supersonic hopes helped knock the wind out of the local economy, and at the tenth anniversary of the

1962 World's Fair the sounds of the struggling economy dampened the celebrations. In addition, Seattle was then more preoccupied with becoming a big-league city through grabbing major-league sports franchises than with building on the arts experience of Century 21.

However, while many locals were groaning over the generally lagging performance of their first big-league team, the Supersonics, others were beginning to enjoy a renaissance of the arts in Seattle — especially in theater. We know now where to look to see the creation at that time of such surviving institutions as the Seattle Rep, Intiman, ACT, and Empty Space theatres as an advertisement for the recurring resilience of our cultural "ups." Even for relative ancients like our Symphony and Art Museum, the nurturing that has flowered since the early and mid-seventies continues to transform these venerable institutions into very good ones. Johnson explains, "You couldn't have great buildings and great endowments without a great organization, and the organizations really grew up from childhood after the 1962 World's Fair. By the time I became the trustee in 1992, while they still had some growing pains, they were maturing nicely into worthy recipients of major funding."

Through its two decades of service the Foundation helped pot and water many of the plants in this flowering of local arts. As often noted here, the artistic activism during the 1990s — both in dollars and ideas — was a reminder of the local can-do attitude that produced two World's Fairs — the Alaska-Yukon-Pacific Exposition of 1909 and Century 21 in 1962. And yet it was also more. During a 1996 interview, ArtsFund President Peter Donnelly advised critic Melinda Bargreen, "This isn't a renaissance; it's a 'naissance.' There has been nothing like this growth in the arts and their capital projects in our region's history."

With its blessed timing, the Kreielsheimer Foundation was able first to join in the building of the core arts groups as effective organizations, and next increasingly help with a great variety of building projects during the heated period of great local wealth. Don Johnson notes, "In the 1990s there were capital challenges every other day. They were legitimate and the timing was right, and I think of the Opera House project as being a kind of symbolic completion of this." Paul Schell, the Seattle mayor who served during those sometimes surreal times, makes a generous analysis of the

Foundation's role: "The late 1990s was a magical period in our city. It nearly built the city's entire cultural infrastructure, almost unlike any other American city. We may call it the Kreielsheimer period."

There is a futurist in Don Johnson that is inclined toward optimism, given the ongoing legacy of the Foundation's many good works — although as a trustee he can no longer write the check that insures it. "There is always going to be something more to do. Now the Seattle Art Museum hopes to expand with a mixed-use high-rise to be built in partnership with Washington Mutual Bank. These advances will go on and on." Philanthropists generally have a right to hope. By having helped to sustain and secure the future vitality of the institutions it endowed, the Kreielsheimer Foundation thereby granted itself a kind of extension by reflection. In its last year the Foundation received the annual Corporate Council for the Arts (now called ArtsFund) Community Achievement Award for "Outstanding Foundation Leadership in the Arts." In his remarks about the value of the award and its recipient, Peter Donnelly also looked forward. "This Foundation came on at the beginning of our golden era for the arts, and has reached out into so many areas of the community. Its impact will be felt for a long time to come."

Support for the arts is motivated by admiration as well as the desire to assist and the pleasure of association. Unlike institutions such as banks, who are looking for partners in investment, patrons of the arts seek excellence in performance, and they may ask for no more. Two of our finest qualities as bipeds with opposing fore-thumbs and creative intelligence are that we can stand up and hold a bow over four strings. Another is that we are attracted to anyone who can rub the one over the other and produce a sound that is transporting. That is, we delight in the virtuosity of others. It is an admiration that helps us transcend many of our ordinary foibles, most importantly envy. While we may enjoy playing "air violin" to the recordings of Heifetz or Mutter, if we also have our wits in hand we do not mistake our playing for theirs. How many, while patronizing the Seattle Symphony, have imagined Gerard Schwarz calling them from the audience to take the baton for a rousing encore of some chestnut like "The Star Spangled Banner"? It has happened, but when it is over the guest conductor returns to his or her seat thrilled yet also knowing that it was the players who did the leading. So in addition to the pleasures of being in the company of artistic excellence, art patronage may also delight in associations with status and celebrity. And whether promoted or not artists are the most deserving of celebrity, because we understand that their popularity is bound to their expressive skills and not to how well or curiously they live or to their capacity to tell a good story—unless their art is writing.

Of course this alluring aura of celebrity gained by one's expressive excellence is fundable. Support for the arts extends from purchasing a discounted ticket to the entire sum of the Kreielsheimer legacy. Artists are the ones—to borrow again from Beverly Sills—who evoke color from what might otherwise seem like another unremarkable unfolding of the gray scale, and that is ordinarily enough. The colors of celebrity cannot match those of the art itself. Consequently the patron does not need to invite the artist to dinner in order to feel repaid. Rather, there is a kind of disinterested wisdom in the fellowship of patron and artist. By loving and supporting the arts one takes part in a culture's enduring traditions.

In great cityscapes it is first the buildings that are remembered and then the developers. Therefore it is a wise developer who chooses a good architect before he or she puts their name on the building. And it is a fortunate culture that is supported by intelligent philanthropy—for no matter what the age or the politics of a culture, it is the fine art that endures. It was to this tradition that Leo and Greye Kreielsheimer wished to make a permanent contribution, and as we have noted it was those established stalwarts—opera, classical music, ballet, theater—that most attracted them. It is to this grand tradition that their chosen trustees, Charles Osborn and Don Johnson, also gave so well.

The work of the Kreielsheimer Foundation will be remembered in halls and practice rooms and promenades. It will be thanked for grooming talents and helping to mature performers by turning a family's wealth to the good work of nourishing the fine and often splendidly impractical arts. The Foundation has made rescues, funded expensive capital improvements and sometimes even operating expenses, given generous endowments, and occasionally even purchased artworks and supported individual artists.

It is in art itself, the performances and exhibits as well as in the teaching and even rehearsing of it, that the life of the arts is revealed, and this is also true of the contributions of the Foundation. Every piece and every performance produced and/or exhibited by an artist or institution supported by Kreielsheimer is part of its endowment. The Foundation's legacy endures in addition within the loving memories that are the time-binders of culture as much as of families, and chronicles like this one are written to capture and hold on to some of these memories so that they may be shared and returned to through the richness of reading.

In summing up the Foundation's endowment to the community, its greatest accomplishment may lie in the funds it granted to the young, for the artistic child is a gift to the future. Listening to Don Johnson tell the story of his first visit to the completed Kreielsheimer Promenade in June 2003, we can

Left to right: Mark Reddington (architect), Deborah Sussman (interior designer), Kathryn Gustafson (landscape architect), Leni Schwendinger (lighting specialist), and Dottie Johnson at the opening of McCaw Hall

hear the inspired child in the trustee as well. "It was black tie but it was public — the first public opening of McCaw Hall. The performance started at 8 p.m., and the part on stage began with the grand singing of Jane Eaglen. She was the first person to utter a note for the public from that stage. The stage performances lasted only an hour because, after all, the new Hall was itself a performer that night and we had all come to also wander around and look the place over. It was so exciting that Dottie and I stayed until midnight when we went out to the Promenade and discovered Jane Eaglen, the person who many consider to be the greatest living Wagnerian soprano, frolicking in Kathryn Gustafson's fountain. Gustafson, scrim designer Leni Schwendinger, and interior designer Deborah Sussman were also wading in the water with her. Now when Dottie took off her shoes and joined them I reached for my camera. Of course none of them were really getting very wet, for the fountain is a thin sheet of water that

Olivia Kreielsheimer, ca. 1985

runs evenly over the west side of the promenade. It is a technique that Gustafson uses very effectively. And I also stepped in — but I kept my shoes on." Throughout his trusteeship, it might well be said that Johnson knew precisely how to both "step in" and "keep his shoes on" as he served the arts and the generous intentions of Leo and Greye Kreielsheimer.

Finally, it is from someone who may be described as the Foundation's "first child," Greye and Leo's late daughter, Olivia, that we learn with authority what her parents would have thought of all the above. Don Johnson is rightfully cheered by the memory of Olivia telling him more than once, "Daddy would have been so proud."

Afterword

In June 2004 Don Johnson joined Peter Donnelly for the joint dedication of the Peter F. Donnelly Arts and Literature Collection and the Kreielsheimer Performance Room at the new main branch of the Seattle Public Library. The event featured some reflections from one of the namesake honorees himself, Peter Donnelly. His remarks are reprinted here.

"I remember at the time that the Kreielsheimer Foundation was approaching its sunset in 2000 one of the newspapers ran a story that said if archaeologists far in the future studied the buildings of this region they would have a lot of questions to answer regarding the Kreielsheimer foundation. They would see the name time and again on buildings all over town. They'd realize pretty quickly that all the buildings the names were attached to have to do with culture. It would also hit them that this Kreielsheimer Foundation must have been one of the most important and ubiquitous forces in the region's cultural life during what will surely be recognized as the golden age for the arts. They would be right in all those conclusions.

"As most of you know, Leo and Greye Kreielsheimer set up their foundation so it would accomplish their wishes and then sunset after twenty-five years. They felt that if it ran longer than that it would become too distant from understanding their objectives. They would, I think, be both gratified and a bit astonished at the legacy the foundation has left. The range of activities the Foundation funded over that time is remarkable. It has included performing arts, visual arts, outdoor sculpture, and cultural parks; arts education at colleges, schools, and universities; arts education at the K-12 level; performing arts centers; general operating support (as through ArtsFund); a variety of other activities with links to the Foundation's purpose, and, very importantly, endowments that will carry the purpose forward within many cultural organizations.

"That gives you some idea of the range of the Foundation. I don't intend to run down the full list of all the grants they've made—we would be here until tomorrow—but I do want to give a few highlights so that you have a sense of the scope and impact. Total grants to some of the top recipients include: $19 million to the City of Seattle for arts facilities, about $11 million each to Seattle Opera, Cornish College, and the Seattle Symphony, $6 million to the Seattle Rep, $4.5 million each to the Seattle Art Museum and ACT, and $3.5 million to both ArtsFund and Pacific Northwest Ballet. Much of this went toward capital campaigns. There are few new buildings or significant expansions and remodels between 1975 and 2000 that did not benefit from Kreielsheimer funds. The Foundation also supported season-long operations, special initiatives, and purchase of sculpture and artwork for important public sites and museums.

"In an arts community that can only trace its origins back a hundred years, endowments were only a much talked about but far-off dream, always at the end of the needs list. The Kreielsheimer Foundation had a major hand in changing that thinking. By its commitment to an endowment program, the Foundation turned what had been discussion to reality. The Foundation directly invested some $16.5 million in endowments to nearly a dozen cultural organizations. These include the Intiman Theatre, Pacific Northwest Ballet, Seattle Art Museum, Seattle Opera, ACT, the Rep, the Seattle Symphony, Cornish, ArtsFund, and a number of institutions of higher education.

"All these grants were made thoughtfully and strategically. From the list of recipients I've mentioned, I suspect most of you know how effectively the funds have been put to use. This is no accident, and you could see why if you knew the first trustee, Charles Osborn, or if you know Charlie's successor, Don Johnson, and the way he works.

"I first got to know Don Johnson when he became trustee of the Foundation after the death of Charlie Osborn. Don was designated to assume the responsibilities of the Foundation and it must have seemed like a monumental assignment, as he was stepping into the middle of a very developed arts community. It is a testimony to him that he became a student in every way, and that in a very short period of time he became one of the true experts on understanding how the arts work, understanding their needs and their aspirations. During the life of the Foundation, while working with the trustees of SeaFirst Bank and subsequently of its new owners Bank of America, Don Johnson parleyed the assets to the point that, by the time it sunseted in 2000, they had distributed a hundred million dollars. It is a truly remarkable story.

"Don kept very much in tune with the day-to-day working of our community and refreshed his knowledge every year by participating in the annual allocations of ArtsFund. I think that it is accurate to say that had Don Johnson not assumed the leadership of the Foundation that the effects of it would have been much narrower than it ultimately was and that the net effect would have been considerably less. It is a point of simple arithmetic. Don spread a lot of money to a lot of groups and much of that money required matching funds, so the effect was very often doubled.

In addition to the endowment that Don placed with the ArtsFund, he gifted the Century Building, a wonderful, four-story building on lower Queen Anne Hill, which is our headquarters and the home as well of Classical KING radio. It was a truly remarkable gift.

"During the years of working together, Don, in addition to being a valued colleague, became a valued friend. Please help me welcome, and join me in a toast to Don Johnson in celebration of him and his work with the Kreielsheimer Foundation."

Appendix
Kreielsheimer Foundation
Grant Recipients

A Contemporary Theater

Admiral Theatre

Alaska Dance Theatre

Alaska Native Heritage Center

Alaska Pacific University

Alice B. Theater

Anchorage Concert Association

Anchorage Museum of History
and Art

Annex Theatre

Annie Wright School

Arboretum Foundation

Archives of American Art

ARCS Foundation, Inc.

Artist Trust

Artists Unlimited

ArtsWest

Bainbridge Island Chamber Music
Festival

Bathhouse Theater

Bellevue Arts Museum

Bellevue Philharmonic Orchestra

Book-It Repertory Theatre

Broadway Center for the
Performing Arts

Bush School

Business Volunteers for the Arts

Capitol Theater

Center on Contemporary Art

Centrum

Child Hearing League

Children's Home Society of
Washington

Children's Hospital Foundation
(Children's Orthopedic Hospital)

City Club

Clymer Museum of Art

Co-Motion Dance

Conbela Associates

Cornish College of the Arts (other
than scholarships)

Cornish College of the Arts (scholarships)

Corporate Council for the Arts /
ArtsFund

Early Music Guild

Empty Space Theatre

Epiphany School

Evergreen State College

Federal Way Philharmonic

Forest Ridge School

Fred Hutchinson Cancer Research
Center

Gonzaga University

Group Theater

Harlequin Productions

Henry Art Gallery

International District Village Square

International Music Festival Seattle

Intiman Theatre

John Stanford International School

KCTS Association

Kirkland Performance Center

Koahnic Broadcast Corporation

Kodiak Baranof Productions, Inc. (Kodiak Arts Council)

KUOW Radio Signal Improvement Project

Ladies Musical Club

Lakeside School

Langston Hughes Performing Arts Center

Lighthouse for the Blind

Maritime Heritage Foundation

Mount Baker Theatre Center

Museum of Flight

Museum of Glass

Museum of History and Industry

Museum of Northwest Art

National Arts Stabilization Fund (Seattle Project)

National Multiple Sclerosis

A New City Theatre and Art Center

911 Media Arts Center

Nordic Heritage Museum

Northwest Asian American Theater

Northwest Boy Choir of Seattle

Northwest Chamber Orchestra

Northwest Hospital Foundation

Northwest Puppet Center

Northwest School

Northwest School for Hearing Impaired Children

Northwest Sinfonietta

On the Boards

Orchestra Seattle / Seattle Chamber Singers

Overlake School

Pacific Lutheran University

Pacific Northwest Ballet

Pacific Science Center

Pantages Centre

Performance Circle

Performance Support Services

Performing Arts Festival, Eastside

Perseverance Theatre

Pike Place Market / Market Foundation

Pilchuck Glass School

Pratt Fine Art Center

Pratt Museum (Homer Society of Natural History, Inc.)

Resource Foundation

Saint Martin's College (now St. Martin's University)

Seattle, City of

Seattle (City of) Center Foundation

Seattle (City of) Center Academy

Seattle Academy

Seattle Art Museum

Seattle Chamber Music Festival

Seattle Children's Home

Seattle Children's Museum

Seattle Children's Theatre

Seattle Chinese Garden

Seattle Community College

Seattle Foundation

Seattle Goodwill

Seattle International Children's Festival

Seattle Jewish Community Center

Seattle Men's Chorus

Seattle, Mime Theatre

Seattle Opera Association (Seattle Opera Endowment)

Seattle Pacific University

Seattle Public Library

Seattle Repertory Theatre

Seattle School District / Alliance for Education

Seattle Symphony

Seattle University

Seattle Young Artists Music Festival

Seattle Youth Symphony Orchestra

Seward Park Art Studio

Sheldon Jackson College

Southeast Effective Development, Inc.

Spectrum Dance Theater

Steamer *Virginia V* Foundation

Tacoma Actors Guild

Tacoma Art Museum

Tacoma Little Theatre

Tacoma Opera

Tacoma Philharmonic

Tacoma Symphony

Tacoma Youth Symphony

Taproot Theatre

Town Hall Association

UMO Ensemble

University Preparatory Academy

University of Puget Sound / School of Music

University of Washington

University of Washington / Burke Museum

University of Washington Press

University of Washington TV Production

Village Theatre

Virginia Mason Medical Foundation

Visual Arts Center of Alaska

Washington Art Consortium

Washington State

Washington Art Commission

Western Washington University / Western Foundation

Western Washington Forest Industries Museum

Whidbey Island Center for the Arts

Whitman College

Whitworth College

Wing Luke Asian Museum

Woodland Park Zoo

Xelfer for *Reflex* magazine

Yakima Valley Museum

YMCA of Seattle and King County

Zion Preparatory Academy

Index

Page numbers referring to illustrations appear in italics.